Hired!

Hired!

HOW TO GET THE ZIPPY GIG.
INSIDER SECRETS FROM A TOP RECRUITER.

Sheila Musgrove

ISBN-: 1523479248
ISBN-13: 9781523479245
Library of Congress Control Number: 2016900955
CreateSpace Independent Publishing Platform
North Charleston, South Carolina

Dedication

For My Mom & Dad: Betty & Gene Musgrove, with Love.

I won the parent lottery with you two. I've had a lifetime of fabulousness from you both – where do I even start?

You taught me what a solid work ethic and truly *showing up* each day means. Thank you for giving me such a strong vision of what it takes to be an entrepreneur and create a successful business.

You taught me that B students could actually do whatever the hell they wanted. You gave me my first speaking gig – perhaps that's where this path all started? You helped me to write my first story in grade 4.

You've been my biggest fans with unwavering support and encouragement in whatever I've chosen to do. (OK, except for that brief dream of being a saxophone player in a rock band – you were right, it probably wasn't the best idea and thank goodness, it was a short lived one. SMILE.)

I'm grateful for a really normal childhood. I know how hard you both worked in your careers to make it really fabulous. As I get older, it amazes me how you did it all.

Two memorable questions you asked me were:

Dad, "*Are you ever going to finish school and get a real job?*" Yes, a reasonable question after a clerk-typist certificate, a Legal Assistant Diploma, and a degree. (And, thank you for attending each one of my convocation ceremonies!)

Mom, said to the 13 year old me, "*You'd better get a really good job because you've got expensive taste and you like clothes and shoes.*" Good advice Mom!

Funny that both questions were about me *finding my fabulous Zippy Gig*!

I'm the luckiest girl in the world to have been blessed with your immense love and support.

Acknowledgements

I have a little secret. I've had a goal of writing a book and being a published author since I was in grade 3. So, I'm over the moon to have achieved that long-standing goal!

I'd like to thank some really special people:

Kim Duke, Sales Diva extraordinaire – who knew that after meeting a decade ago that we'd be wrapping up this little project? Thank you for helping me to find my fun, sassy and "real" writing voice, which is a hell of a lot more fun than the fork-in-the-eye writer voice that I started with! Thank you for your endless rounds of edits, firm deadlines and support. I think you're right – there just might be another book on the horizon for me to write. Lady, what have you started? GRIN.

The amazing people who gave their time, professional perspective and trust to be quoted in the book: Cory Woron, Tim Tamashiro, The Style Guys: Jason Krell & Alykhan Velji, Kirstey Ball, Todd Hirsch, Frank Lonardelli, James M. Bond, Dion Kostiuk, Shelley Vandenberg, Carol Ionel, Mark Smye, Chris Day, Darin Wyatt, Mark Breslaw, Paula Breeze, Sean Sandhurst, Sue Wood, Janice Webster and Paul Trudel, I'm beyond grateful for your insight and contributions.

My fabulous team: Rachelle Enns, Aaron Mitchell & Mark Warawa. Thank you for finding the humour, fun and reward in what we do every day. It takes talent, insight, curiosity, an incredible memory and a massive attention span to be a great recruiter – you've all got it. Thank you for being part of the TAG story and for sharing the secret formulas with your candidates. Thank you for "taking names and doing stuff" ☺. And, for bubble wrap, champagne and celebrations. May there be an abundance of all three!

To my longstanding clients – thank you for support and continuing to turn to TAG to assist in finding stellar talent for your teams. I'm beyond grateful.

To the thousands of candidates who I've had the pleasure of working with - thank you for each one of those disastrous interviews! GRIN. Your deer-in-the-headlights responses to my interview questions gave me the inspiration to figure out how to make resume writing and interviewing easy and painless....for both of us. After seeing your "ah ha" moments when it was all explained made me realize that this information was somewhat golden. It's been incredibly rewarding to work with all of you who did the hard work to make a shiny resume filled with sexy results and made the time to be well-rehearsed to deliver a kick-ass interview. I wish that you could see how dramatically your confidence soared throughout the process. I love hearing the excitement in your voice when I share the news that you got the zippy gig!

Thank you for helping to make this sexy-ass book a reality! GRIN.

My heartfelt thanks,

Sheila

Introduction:

Are you ready to learn how to get
HIRED and get the *Zippy Gig*?

The burning question you're probably thinking – *What the hell is a **Zippy Gig***?
The word **zippy** is used frequently in my office. Who doesn't smile when saying the
word ZIPPY?

Zippy Gigs are part of my fun, silly language. My thinking? Why use dull words when
there are far more sparkly ones to use?

When you give something a **sassy** name, like *Zippy*, the task is just waaaay more fun to
tackle. (And I think it has definitely helped me create one of the hottest recruitment
firms in Canada.)

When my team is doing business development research – which as we all know – can
be a little dull, it's way more fun to say,

"I'm working on finding new *Zippy Gigs.*"

So the name just seemed to be a natural fit for the book.

Who wouldn't want a job that you'd describe as a ZIPPY GIG?

The idea of writing a resume and going on interviews might feel daunting. Rest as-
sured, I'm going to make the process of being **HIRED** and getting the **Zippy Gig** beyond fun for you.

So let's get the *Zippy* started.

So, you've been searching the business aisle of the book store in search of some sage advice. (And we all know how cheesy and DULL most career books are!)

Well, GREAT news.

This isn't your average, dull, mind-numbing, HR type of book on resumes and interviews.

You're going to **DITCH EVERYTHING** you've ever learned about writing a resume and toss it out the window.

You're going to learn step by step *how to write a kick-ass resume* that gets your phone ringing for interviews *for your Zippy Gig.* I mean really, what recruiter says the word **ASS** before we even get started?!

I'll Show You My Insider Secrets.

And just how do I know the *Insider Secrets* and what you need to get hired?

I've been in Agency Recruitment for close to 20 years. I launched my own firm TAG Recruitment Group in 2005. During the last decade I've de-coded what makes a resume kick-ass and *shiny* and what makes a winning interview.

As I did more interviews, it became increasingly obvious that most candidates were lost in the dark when it came to resumes and interviews. **I mean LOST.**

I put together a formula for kick-ass shiny resumes for my candidates and then...

THE MAGIC STARTED HAPPENING.

The results were immediate.

My candidates were more confident with their finished resume and excited to deliver an out-of-the-park interview. Thousands of candidates have taken my one on one coaching to secure their *Zippy Gig*.

I'm super excited to take the lessons learned from those interviews and break it down into an easy to use format for you.

I guarantee the formula to create a shiny new resume is **easy**.

I hope you'll have a chuckle or two – you might even *spill your coffee or martini,* through the process.

You'll end with a shiny resume that gets your phone ringing with opportunity.

Before we dive in – I'd love to tell you a few glossy details about my company TAG.

I've grown my company from a crazy idea in my head to a thriving multi-million dollar recruitment agency.

The name TAG Recruitment came about while zipping down the highway one afternoon. I was toying with calling my firm, Musgrove Recruitment, but seriously, how dull would that have been?

I had an epiphany – recruitment is like the childhood game of TAG.

We find where the best candidates are *hiding* – seek them out and when we find them, TAG, they are it!

One of our tag lines is, **Where are you hiding? We'd really like to find you! TAG.**™

My company and I have been very honoured to receive some very shiny awards over the years:

- PROFIT & Chatelaine's W100 ranking of the Top 100 Women Entrepreneurs in Canada. (We've appeared on this one 4 times!)

- Red Deer College – Distinguished Alumnus (I did my initial post secondary at this amazing school. I'm a very proud Alum.)

- Alberta Venture's Fast Growth 50 ranking of the fastest growing companies in Alberta. Delighted to make the list 5 times and counting.

- Calgary Chamber of Commerce awarded TAG with the Emerging Entrepreneur of the Year in our early days! We even had a film crew follow us for a few days to shoot a video. OK - that made me feel a bit like a rock star!

- PROFIT Hot 50 ranking of the hottest 50 start ups in Canada. That was a very cool moment too.

TAG just celebrated 10 years in business – a milestone that I'm really proud to have achieved.

I had to pinch myself that it's been a decade already.

We booked a restaurant and threw a splashy party to celebrate with our amazing clients and friends.

My Mom hugged everyone in the room....at least once. My Dad smiled the entire night.

My amazing team gave me the best gift ever:

A basket filled with *Pringles* (doesn't everyone LOVE Pringles), *Cheez Whiz* and a fabulous bottle of scotch.

I shared the Pringles, but the Cheez Whiz and scotch came home with me. GRIN.

Let's get to work and get YOU into a fabulous new *ZIPPY GIG.*

You're going to write a shiny kick-ass resume AND, you're going to be uber-prepared to deliver an off the charts, rock star type of interview.

You'll be the interviewee they drool over.

You'll walk into ANY interview exuding confidence.

The idea of bringing 2-3 resume pages to life will have you bursting with excitement.

Yes, sunshine, **bursting.**

You'll be beyond prepared and you'll have the insight of knowing what a hiring manager wants to hear in an interview.

Imagine walking out of your next interview on Cloud 9, knowing you've aced the interview. (Yes, that will be you.)

This book contains not only how to write a shiny kick-ass resume and how to rock an interview. I'll show you all the nuts and bolts in between. I'll also share the downright silly things that can have a star candidate sent straight to the recycle bin.

 Sassy Sheila Note: When you see this **Shiny S symbol,** it's an alert of 1 of 3 things: This is *super-important, super Sassy Sheila ahead,* or it could be a warning **that I'm about to use the word Sexy. More on that one later. (Smile.)**

"The secret to getting started is getting started."

— MARK TWAIN

CHAPTER 1

Let's Get *Zippy*

There's lots of reasons why you might be looking for a new *Zippy Gig*.

Do You Fit One of These Scenarios?

You've Been Laid Off:

If you've been through a lay off – you'll likely be feeling terrified of being without work and an income.

The uncertainty of how long it will take to find a new role is unsettling and unnerving for sure.

And, the last thing you want is fear seeping through in an interview! (And, believe me, hiring managers and recruiters can sense fear.)

You're Not Growing. And You're Bored To Death In Your Job:

You're in a situation where you're simply *bored to tears* in your current role. You've tackled every challenge in the role and you're ready for new challenges.

Do you feel like you're being paid to watch paint dry?

That's what it can feel like when you aren't being challenged. Or maybe you just don't have enough to do.

You're looking to be on the edge of your seat and feeling excited again!

Your Job Just Isn't The Right Fit:

Are you in a situation where your work environment, day-to-day job duties, boss or colleagues don't align with what makes you happy?

Perhaps your ideas are being squashed, or creativity isn't encouraged – **maybe the carpet smells** – it doesn't matter.

Something just doesn't feel right for you and you're ready to exit stage left.

I interviewed a candidate who chose to leave her company as her boss would actually throw things. Seriously! She drew the line at a laptop being tossed her way.

Yes, we're happy to report, she's now with a nice organization with a **firm "no throwing" policy**! The only things they throw at her are compliments.

You've Been Let Go:

Oh dear. That's a tough one. I've dedicated an entire chapter to dealing with the **BIG T**. If this is you, zip over to **Chapter 6**. Trust me, it'll make you feel better.

You're Going Back to Work OR Starting Your Career:

After taking time off, you've decided it's time to go back to work. Or, perhaps you've finished school and you're looking for your first exciting new gig. I'll share lots of ways to make your skills and background a stand out.

We're going to walk through finding your new *Zippy Gig* together.

And, once you know what the heck to put on a resume and how to get through an interview with confidence and ease, you'll be GRINNING ear to ear!

Candidates I've worked with walk out of my office like they've been handed a secret code. Yes, grinning ear to ear. And, a wee bit of disbelief on how easy it all is.

That'll be you too!

Ready to Dive In?

"Kid, you'll move mountains."

— DR. SEUSS

CHAPTER 2

Send Your Rusty Resume to the Recycle Bin

After all of the thousands of resumes I've read, I think there must be a really bad book out there that has everyone doing the wrong things.

Everyone is writing the same dull, boring resume. WE need to find that boring resume book and bury it. (Or, maybe we should keep the secrets to writing shiny resumes just between us.)

I'm going to be BOLD here.

BORING RESUMES DON'T GET RESULTS.

I call BORING resumes RUSTY. Yes, they're old and rusty.

RUSTY defined:
> "Faded or shabby; impaired by time" (Source: Dictionary.com)

**The plain truth – if your resume is boring
(and impaired by time) your phone won't be ringing.**

Here's a FACT that may shock you...

"80% of resumes are rejected in less than 11 seconds."

PETER HARRIS, FINANCIAL POST
SEPTEMBER 8, 2015

Your resume at first viewing will get only
11 SECONDS max.

Yes, that's it.

Let me ask you – **what percentile does your resume fall in?**

Are you part of the **80% being sent to the recycle bin**? Or the **elite 20%** that make it through the first cut in those first 11 seconds?

If I was a betting woman, I'd guess you're in that **DREADED 80% pile.**

Here's the **GREAT** news.

I'm going to share with you the Insider SECRETS so YOU _will be_ in the elite 20% in those first 11 seconds.

Want to know how resumes are actually read?

Remember the last trashy or sci-fi novel you read? You devoured every delectable word. Eagerly flipping pages, and not missing a *single* detail in the fabulous story.

You might think your resume gets read EXACTLY that same way.

Word by word by word.

WRONG. Not a chance.

Everyone thinks that's how they're read, *so you're in good company.*

Employers & Recruiters Read Your Resume Like *People* Magazine

Resumes are read a bit like how you'd scan *People* magazine while waiting in the line at the grocery store.

While you're in line, you might give the entire magazine four minutes. You're after the juicy stuff. That's it.

You SKIM.

That's really how employers and recruiters read resumes too. Skimming for the JUICY stuff.

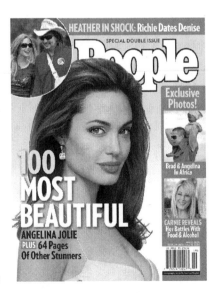

Who has time to read an entire *People* magazine?

Four minutes brings us up to date on the comings and goings of all our favourite celebrities.

You get 11 SECONDS to highlight the "comings and goings" of your career.

Will I Buy YOU, or Chatelaine or Men's Health?

When you skim through *People* magazine at the grocery store, you decide after 4 minutes if you're buying the magazine or moving on to Chatelaine or Men's Health.

After 11 seconds, *I'm deciding if I'm buying your resume.*   (And, by "buying", I mean picking up the phone to have a conversation with you.)

6 Surprising Things that Get ZERO Attention in the 11 Second First Cut.

1. Career Summary:

Yes, it's true. We don't look at those well thought out and crafted words that describe how **AMAZING** you are. (I'm sure you're amazing, we just need to show your AMAZINGNESS in other *CLEVER* ways.)

Why? 11 seconds.

2. Career Highlights:

Assume that everything on the top part of your resume doesn't get read. And, even if there are numbers, they'll likely get missed.

3. Target Position:

Very unlikely it will be read unless it's to the point and names a specific role. **Less is more to get attention**.

4. Mind-numbing bullets:

The long list of bullet points listed under each role that describe what your functional responsibilities were in each job. **Nope, not reading those**. *(Stay with me. I'll show you how to replace those bullets with impactful, concise detail that WILL get read.)*

5. Interests:

The exception is if you have written something *INTERESTING*.

One way to be interesting is to be unusual. One of the recruiters I hired wrote that one of his interests was Dodgeball. That little quirk made me laugh and I picked up the phone to call him.

Why? Because it was something I'd never seen on a resume. And, well, who doesn't smile when remembering Dodgeball from grade school?

6. References:

They don't get noticed at first glance of your resume.

The 11 Second Skim:

You're likely scratching your head wondering **what the heck gets read in those quick 11 seconds?** Hiring managers and recruiters are professional skimmers. We're great speed readers. Based on the sheer volume of resumes received, we can only SKIM. It's all about the skimming in those **quick 11 seconds**.

The 5 Things That <u>ARE</u> SKIMMED:

Skim #1: Your current and last few positions: Company name and your job titles.

Job titles tell us very quickly what kind of role and level you've been working at previously. In a nano-second it tells us if previous roles would align to the role we're looking to fill.

Skim #2: Start and end dates (*and hint we're looking for GAPS in dates – you might have run off to the circus or been unemployed – either way, we want to know. More on this later.*)

Skim #3: Education. We're looking for levels – college, university, post graduate, professional development. If a certain educational level is required for the role, that might be the first thing we look at to see if you qualify.

Skim #4: A quick glance back up to the top to check **where you're located.**

Skim #5: Numbers & percentages will likely always get a quick glance if they're in the body of the resume. **More on #'s and %'s in a bit.**

There you go. That's what 11 seconds gets you.

Tick Tock
11 Seconds Zips by in a Flash

The New Rules of Resumes:
From RUSTY to SUPER SHINY

Don't settle for a rusty resume. There isn't a second to waste in keeping that old rusty thing.

You've got 11 seconds. A rusty resume is a fast track to the recycle bin.

No call.
No interview.
No job.

The SHINY chain is an absolute STANDOUT. It is polished, shiny and glistens and stands out amongst the big pile of rusty chains. Employers and recruiters LOVE SHINY.

Which one would you pick in your 11 seconds?

The shiny one of course.

I've always loved all things SHINY.

Men like shiny cars, shiny golf clubs, shiny shoes.

Women like just about anything shiny.

When the sun hits an object, it glistens when it's shiny and catches your eye.

That's what we're going to do to your resume. Make it stand out when the sun (those 11 seconds) are shining on your resume.

The definition of **SHINY:**

> **"Bright or glossy.** Something that is great, neat, very cool,
> (Dictionary.com)

A shiny resume is all about YOUR RESULTS.

It will be all about the *amazing, impressive things you've done.*

Your new SUPER SHINY resume will be great, neat and very cool, just like the definition.

Before we move into SHINY, let's see if your resume passes the rusty test.

4 Signs You Have A Rusty Resume:

- I've sent out hundreds of resumes and I'm not getting any calls.

- I have no idea why I'm not getting calls as my experience is EXACTLY what they are asking for.

- I'm following up on my resume, but no one is returning my call.

- Zero job action. Period.

The Verdict: Your resume IS RUSTY.

Guess what we see resume after resume?

A long list of **MIND-NUMBING bullets** that describe your functional responsibilities.

This is what I call a BORING, OLD SCHOOL RESUME.

 **It's RUSTY.   And it's really hurting you in today's competitive job market.**

Your resume is probably like a rusty old bucket. It is filled with holes. It certainly doesn't hold water. Sure, it is still a bucket. It just doesn't work as well as it used to. Kind of like all of those resumes you're sending out – **they're part of the 80%**, leaking out the bottom and not helping you get a job. Not one bit.

Here's A Chunk Of A Boring, RUSTY Resume: Don't Do This At Home

ABC Company, Account Executive   **2012 – Present**
- Responsible for cold calling
- Did networking and marketing as required
- Sold many new accounts in the Calgary area.
- Wrote proposals and met with clients.
- Handled objections

The old style resume is a real job killer and the fastest way to be in the 80% REJECT pile.

Why?

You're back to the BORING list of bullets that describe what you were responsible for in each role.

Do I actually read those bullets?

Not a chance.

Because there's **RARELY** anything worth reading.

We just skip them.

This worn out old formula makes your resume look like every other resume out there.

Even worse is if you're using Times New Roman font. 99.9% of resumes use it.

OK, are you with me here? Rusty isn't working.

But **here's the GREAT news** – you're going to learn how your resume can be a knock out in 11 seconds.

From RUSTY to SHINY.

You'll be glistening in 11 seconds.

The *secrets* are in Chapter 4 and the *big magic* is in Chapter 5.

CHAPTER 3

The Bones of Your
Super Shiny Resume

Let's **ease** into this task of creating your shiny resume.

It's a bit like avoiding going to the gym.

The hard part is getting your ass out the door. Once you're out, you're on your way.
You always feel great once it's done.

But getting started can feel like the hard part. Believe me, I get it.

It's like we're going to go on a *tour of the gym*, but not actually work out. (The sweat
is going to come in the next chapter...)

But till then, **let's talk about the BONES - the big picture.**

"Everything stinks till it's finished."

— DR. SEUSS

So let's get stinky!

5 Shiny Resume Bones To Get You Started:

Let's look at the bones of a shiny resume. Good bones give your shiny new resume a solid structure.

1. RESUME LENGTH:

If you're just out of high school or college, 1 page is fine. Once you have a few years of experience, you should aim for 2 – maximum 3 pages.

Experienced professionals with at least 5 years experience should *always* be longer than 1 page. If it is only 1 page, you've likely missed adding your successes. We'll talk about the importance of outlining successes - "the magic" in the next chapter.

And, I'll be dashing back to my printer looking for the rest of your resume. (Yes – I can really dash in stilettos!)

2. CHRONOLOGICAL – And, how far back?

Your resume should always be **chronological**. Grouping roles by skill or job type make it a bit like trying to read a bowl of alphabet soup.

Your most recent employment first and then work backwards.

You don't need to go back to the beginning of time.

Go back 10 years or to high school.

You can go back further if a role falls in the middle of that 10 year mark. I certainly don't recommend going back further than 15 years.

And, if you think about it, your skills and experience from the last 10 years is more in line with the type of job you're seeking now, vs. the type of role you were doing 15 or 20 years ago.

I loved the 80's. The big hair. The ridiculous fashions. The cool music.

But, it was a longgggggggg time ago. And, frankly so were the 60's and 70's. I coach candidates to take off *any reference* to a date from the 80's or earlier. Why? Well, my recruiters all were born somewhere in the 80's. Soooo, you're likely going to remind them of their mom or dad. And, mom or dad might not be right for the gig.

3. What FONT SIZES Should You Use?

Your name: 14 – 16 (bold)

Resume categories: 12 – 14 (bold)

Company name & Titles: 12 (bold)

Resume content: 10 – 11

Different font sizes and bolding help the reader to ***visually understand*** your resume sections.

Anything over a 16 font is just YELLING.
A 9 font or smaller is *WHISPERING*.

4. FORMATTING: How To Avoid Sending Your Resume Into The Black Hole:

If you're uploading to a resume capture system, (called an ATS or an Applicant Tracking System) a few things will have it *disappear into thin air* before it is even read.

You really don't want that.

3 Silly Formatting Things You Want To Avoid:

1. Putting your contact details into a text box – what can happen is that it simply tells the system there's absolutely nothing to see! And, voila, you're lost *forever*.

2. Filling your resume with text boxes for the content or various sections – it ends up looking like alphabet soup more often than not.

3. PDF files often don't convert well. So, a good Word.doc is the best route.

Additional Formatting Recommendations:

- **Avoid putting borders** around your resume or heavy formatting. Start with a blank Word document and we'll build from there.

- When you're using a header, **use the actual header** for formatting. If you guess where the header should fall on the second page....well, you've just told the recruiter you could use a brush up on Word as you don't know how to insert a header. (Yikes!)

- **Photos of your gorgeous face shouldn't appear.** However, an exception would be if you're in an industry where your look is part of the position. One example I recently encountered was for an interior design role. Her look was part of her brand and how she marketed her services. It worked.

- **Select a font other than Times New Roman!** Stand out with Calibri, Tahoma or Arial.

- **Never use the comic font for your resume.** Yes, true, we have seen it many times. We're not looking for Spiderman.

5. YOUR CONTACT DETAILS: Let's Start At The Top

- Your name. Use the name you wish to be called. If your name is Robert, but you answer to Bob, use Bob. Use the name you answer to on daily basis.

- Your formal legal name is only required on your payroll forms. There's no need to use your middle name on your resume – just a first and last name.

- Your home address doesn't have to be included on the resume. It can be left off for confidentiality reasons.

- You'll absolutely need a phone number – ideally just your cell.

- If you're using a home phone, think about who could be answering (Mom, Dad, Grandma, Grandpa, kids...). You want to limit the number of people between you and that exciting phone call for a pre-screen.

- Your email address should be your first and last name and should display as such. Job searching is the time to amp up your professionalism. Cute email addresses such as cutiepie16@hotmail.com or studguy@yahoo.ca should never be used on a resume. Similarly, your year of birth shouldn't be used as you're just telling the world how old you are. And, no need to spill those beans.

Here's a quick example of your contact info layout:

Bob Smith
403-555-1234
Bob.smith@gmail.com

Let's keep the *zippy* going!

9 SHINY RESUME CATEGORIES: Get Your 11 Seconds Of Sparkle!

 A Very Important & Sassy Sheila Note: We're going to talk about 9 shiny categories, however not all 9 will get attention in the 11 seconds.

Some sections as we've talked about - might *never even get read*, **EVER**.

Let's start with 2 that almost *NEVER* get read:

1. **Career Summary or Highlights:** Can be included, but *assume it won't be read.* If you do include, use it to highlight a very select group of achievements with numbers and/or percentages.

2. **Target Position:** Can be very helpful, but avoid vague generalities, such as: "Seeking a rewarding position with a growing company". That won't get a second of attention.

That doesn't tell me *anything* meaningful.

If you're applying for multiple positions, you'll want to customize for each role. **Be specific.**

LESS is more:

Experienced Administrative professional, seeking an Executive Assistant role.

Strong hunter seeking a Senior New Business Development position.

Experienced Forklift Operator seeking a day shift position.

University graduate seeking an entry level Sales position.

There are 2 sections that MUST appear.

Giving attention to these 2 key shiny areas will ensure your 11 seconds count.

 3. Career History: You're in the 11 second zone!

We always look for the company name and positions on the **left** and the dates aligned on the **right** and in **bold** font.

Here's An Example:

ABC Company, Account Executive   **January 2014 – Present**

Months should always be spelled out, to make your resume more complete. We're looking for consistency in dates as well. When one positions ends, the next one should start. If there *are* gaps - then you need to fill in what you were doing at that point in time.

Following the company name, position title and dates will be a 1 – 3 sentence overview of your role. (More on the "how to" on this one a bit later in the chapter. Keep reading!)

Being able to describe your position in a **succinct manner** is probably the most **valuable exercise in writing a resume as it makes your interview shine! Most people** stumble and ramble all over the place in trying to describe what they do. (Yes, we'll go through the "how to" on this one too!)

If you're an experienced professional, **career history must start on the first page**. If you're a recent college or university graduate, I recommend leading with education *before* career history.

 4. EDUCATION: You're in the 11 Second Zone!

Ah, I've got fond memories of living on a student budget. Instant noodle soup, black coffee and cheap carbs...oh, and my Dad's homemade wine were all staples that got me through school.

Lots of positions have very specific educational requirements. So you'll want to ensure you're highlighting your educational background very clearly.

Start with Post Secondary and work backwards to high school. Chronological order. Post Secondary out ranks high school, so it goes first.

Again, if high school was more than 10 years ago, *do leave off the year of graduation.* If you leave it on you're just sharing how your age. *And, that needs to be kept your little secret.*

Indicate if your degree, diploma or certificate was awarded, otherwise we'll assume you didn't graduate. If you've got the paper and you've donned the cap and gown, be sure everyone knows it.

Here's A Shiny Example of how to display your education:

EDUCATION:

Bachelor of Arts, Major: Business Administration. Degree Awarded, 2010, University of Calgary.

Business Administration, Diploma Awarded, 2009, Red Deer College.

High School Diploma, Diploma Awarded 2007, Harry Collinge High School.

If scholarships were awarded, do include them.

If there are a lot of awards, add a section called, AWARDS. If you received an off the charts GPA, note that detail as well!

 If you've caught a hiring manager or recruiter's attention with your career history and your education, there's a good chance that the following section will get a SKIM.

5. PROFESSIONAL DEVELOPMENT/CERTIFICATIONS/ASSOCIATIONS:

You can use one or all of the above in this category.

Professional Development:
- Include specific courses
- Note specific professional certifications attained.

Professional Associations:
- Include Memberships in Professional Associations

These last 3 sections will get SKIMMED if your resume is in the 20% pile.

6. INTERESTS: Make Sure It's Interesting!

OK – now I'm going to say something that isn't meant to hurt your feelings.

I know you probably have many interests like gardening, cooking, reading, hiking, etc.

They are fun and interesting to YOU but not to an employer or recruiter. Why? It isn't all that interesting to us. We see the same few interests over and over – it doesn't stand out, so we just gloss over.

However, if you've completed 5 marathons, jumped out of an airplane, travelled to several countries, taken cooking classes around the world, self taught a language, etc. *these are* interesting things to an employer or recruiter. One of my recruiters has completed 3 degrees, travelled and lived throughout Asia and taught ESL to kids. That's all cool.

Why? Because they stand out. They're unique and different vs. the same boring stuff that's typically listed.

Think about all of the *really cool stuff* you like to do in your leisure. Give your future employer a little glimpse into what things you find fun. It shows your personality and character and THAT gives you an edge.

7. Volunteer Work: Show Us You Care

Volunteer work should always be included. It is a great way to showcase your philanthropic interests.

Be sure to indicate *how many hours per week* you volunteer, where you've volunteered, specific achievements and accountabilities.

If you've volunteered 10 hours per week for the last 5 years that's a big commitment you'd want to highlight. If you don't share, we could assume you volunteered for 1 hour over the past 5 years.

8. SPORTS ACHIEVEMENTS:

Athletic achievement *should always, always be included*. This is a significant area to have your resume stand out.

Why do we love seeing your sports achievements?

Athletics speak to many soft skills that employers are very interested in such as: teamwork, competitiveness, leadership, desire to win, ability to lose graciously, ability to take on a rigorous training program, commitment and tenacity. These are all amazing skills to bring to a workplace!

There you have it. We've **eased** into the bones of your shiny resume.

You know where the super shiny areas are and you've started to think about what makes those important parts stand out.

It's like you've completed the tour of the gym. You know the lay out.

Now you're going to lace up the runners and get to work.

When you have great work outs, you're going to see results.

And, that's exactly what we're going to talk about next...

Your SEXY Results.

CHAPTER 4

SHINY: Your *Sexy* Results In 2 Quick Steps

 This just might be the first business book to use the word **SEXY** to talk about resumes. Yup, pretty sure.

Numbers, percentages and results ARE *sexy* to employers and recruiters.

They get attention. And *you want attention.*

"There are two possible outcomes: The result confirms the hypothesis, then you've made a measurement.

If the result is contrary to the hypothesis, then you've made a discovery."

— ENRICO FERMI

Read that quote *twice*.

If you say you're GREAT at your job, your results will confirm that hypothesis. Easy.

But if the numbers don't prove you're GREAT at your job, you've just made a discovery on *what else should be measured in your resume.*

I've interviewed countless exceptionally talented candidates who have never considered outlining their *sexy* successes on their resumes.

I interviewed a stand out candidate this past summer. He was a tremendously articulate, professional sales candidate. I skimmed his resume and liked the type of companies he'd worked for, so we set up a time to meet.

At the end of our hour-long meeting I discovered:

- He built a retail portfolio in excess of 4 million dollars annually through building a client base of over 1000 Clients within 2 years.
- He sold uber high end electronics through cold calling up to 40 prospects per day, selling 100K+ systems.
- On a zero entertainment budget, he secured ~900K in new business in less than 1 year.
- He was part of a team that sold fractional ownership of jets in excess of 26 million dollars. How cool is that?

And the list went on. **He was a star...CLEARLY!**

Once we uncovered these amazing results, I looked at him and said,

"Hmmm, do you think I would know about these out-of-the-park results by reading your current resume?" (Insert a big GRIN).

You guessed it.

Not ONE of the above results was on his first draft resume. We sure shone it up after that first meeting!

 Let's dive into making *your resume* sexy with numbers.

And we're going to DITCH the bullets. Yes, it's time.

Are you ready?

You're about to do the shiny 2-Step!

My SHINY 2-Step Resume Formula:

Here's the secret.

Once you nail this 2-STEP formula on your resume, interviews will be EASY.

You'll clearly be able to describe what your roles are/were and you'll be armed with all sorts of sparkling details about your achievements.

A hiring manager is seeking to understand only 2 things:

1. Succinctly, _what_ was your role.

2. How _well_ did you do in each role.

A future company is _buying your previous results and successes._

If you've been successful in each of your past roles, odds are you're planning on continuing to be successful. You're not going to go from being a star to a dud now are you?

Sounds silly, but it's true.

STEP 1: Create a SUMMARY of each role vs. a long list of bullets

It's time for you to get short, sweet and to the point.

Read through your bullets one last time. Now hit the delete button.

POOF, they're gone. I feel better already. You will too.

I'm going to show you exactly how to carefully craft a few sentences that make it super clear what your role is/was.

All you have to do is answer 3 super simple questions to create a succinct step 1 summary.

Your Step 1 Super Simple Questions:

What level did you report to?

What is/was your job?

What was your scope?

When you answer these 3 questions, it will be **crystal clear** what your role entailed.

You've hit the BIG SHINY MOMENT!

Ahhhh.

1. **Example**: Reporting to the Canadian Vice President of Sales, I'm accountable for developing a net new book of business within an assigned territory in Calgary.

2. **Example:** Reporting to the Division Director, I was the Administrative Assistant for the Director and her team of 5 Managers.

3. **Example:** Reporting to the Warehouse Manager, I'm accountable for a team of 20 day shift Material Handlers. Responsible for scheduling, performance management, safety and production.

Do this test to see if you've nailed Step 1:

Read the sentences to Grandma, a 5 year old or even to a good friend.

If they nod their head and say "I had no idea that's what your job was!" – you've hit the jackpot.

If they look glazed over with a look of confusion...or boredom, you haven't hit the point quite yet.

Once you've passed the test, let's move on.

One to three sentences maximum.
Keep it simple and powerful.

Let's get on to the good stuff.

SEXY Step 2!

STEP 2:   Showing your *Sexy* Results

This is *the* SHINY.

This is *the* SEXY.

This is what's going to make your phone ring.

It's *all* about your amazing **RESULTS** and **ACHIEVEMENTS.**

It's *all* about the numbers.

The MAGIC lies in answering 3 BIG questions to create your SEXY results.

**Your Step 2 Super Simple Questions
To Uncover Your Sexy Results:**

How big?

How much?

How many?

Step 2 is all about YOUR KEY SUCCESSES and KEY ACHIEVEMENTS:

Before we dive in, I'm going to give you a few bones on how a finished Step 2 will look.

The Step 2 on your resume is going to have **BULLETS**. (Yes – in this section bullets are GOOD)

SECRET:

Bullets _will get read_ if they're used under a heading that screams:

THERE'S SOMETHING IMPORTANT TO READ HERE.

Employers and recruiters will take note that **there's important stuff to read** if you use one of these **magic headings**:

<u>Key Successes</u> or <u>Key Achievements</u>

You'll bullet each success or achievement.

Why does this work? Simple.

By bolding/underlining the beautiful words above, you're telling the reader there's **sexy**, important, cool, validated stuff to read below the sub heading.

It catches their attention. Big time.

And, while we might still be in the initial SKIM phase of the 11 seconds, you've just put another few seconds into the **SKIM bank account**.

As a recruiter– when I see this stuff I'll slow right down to take in the numbers and percentages you've outlined.

Outlining KEY SUCCESSES/ACHIEVEMENTS in each role tells me you've got a track record of being successful.

Hiring managers and recruiters *want to talk to candidates* who have a history of being successful.

As I've said earlier, a hiring manager is going to buy your previous results.

If you've been successful in the past, odds are you'll find ways to keep being successful.

Wait a second.

Is that your phone I hear ringing?

13 Shiny Success Ideas to get your wheels turning:

 Remember – numbers are *sexy!* Let's create some sexy bullets for you.

Get your pen out and start jotting down all of the areas you've excelled in. Here are some ideas to get the ideas flowing:

1. Attendance – have you had 100% attendance in the last year? Two years? Longer?
2. Accuracy in your work – do you have specific targets for quality? Have you achieved those targets? Or even exceeded?
3. Have you been promoted? Was it in record time?
4. Have you been asked to take on additional responsibilities? If so why?
5. Have you been asked to formally or informally train or mentor others?
6. How well did you do against any measurable targets? (HINT – look at your last performance review if you have one. There are loads of GEMS in those written reviews.)
7. Were you recognized by your peers or leadership with awards or accolades?
8. Did you bring forward any ideas that were implemented?
9. Rankings/grades on any professional development courses.
10. Were you selected for a special project? If so, out of how many people?
11. Where did your performance rank amongst others in the same role?
12. What can you validate with numbers or percentages?
13. What did you do that was above and beyond your basic role?

The ideas should be flowing!

Are you grinning ear to ear? You're probably realizing you've got loads of great results to share. You just never thought of it this way before.

You're probably kicking yourself in the behind for missing these *sexy* shiny details from your resume all of this time.

It's also probably become clear why your phone hasn't been ringing.

If you look up, likely there's a light bulb over your head. GRIN.

11 Shiny Success Ideas If You're New To Your Career:

I've presented what I lovingly call *"The Zippy Gig"* seminar to loads of new college and university graduates over the years.

 When I talk about Step 2 of the resume process, I always see a *little panic* come over their faces. They worry that they don't have any sexy results.

That is, until I share some ways that those new to their careers can shine in Step 2.

Here are some ideas to get your creativity flowing:

1. 100% attendance in the last two years

2. Worked 20 hours per week while maintaining a full course load.

3. Volunteered 10 hours per week for the past year.

4. Secured the Coordinator role out of 200 applicants.

5. Nominated by peers for XX.

6. Achieved a 3.99 GPA.

7. Nominated for the Student of the Year.

8. Recognized with the XX Scholarship.

9. Received the highest grade in XX course out of XX classmates.

10. Consistently exceeded nightly beverage sales goals.

11. Ate 1460 cans of Campbell's soup while in school. Ha – just making sure you're paying attention!

Shiny Success Ideas for Sales Professionals:

If you're in sales and you don't have any numbers or percentages on your resume...

Burn it.

Get out your BBQ lighter and set that resume on fire. Now.

In sales *everything is measured*. If it's measured and it showcases what a star you are, include it.

Here are 8 ideas to get the wheels turning:

1. Built account base from zero to $XX.

2. Grew revenue in assigned accounts from $X to $Y.

3. Rankings within the sales team – ranked #1 out of 150 reps within 6 months.

4. Honoured with Presidents Club for exceeding 2014 plan by 250%

5. Secured 15 new accounts in the first quarter of 2015 exceeding my target by 50%.

6. Nominated by peers for the XX award!

7. Won a 2.5 Million RFP, representing the largest win in Canada in 2016.

8. Promoted to Senior Account Executive within 6 months.

Here's What A SHINY Resume Looks Like!

 When you put the 2-step formula together, the result is a crisp, clear shiny resume with **sexy** results.

It is easy to read and understand.

I know immediately that you've been successful.

Here's a Shiny Resume Example:

ABC Company, Account Executive   **January 2014 – Present**

Reporting to the Canadian Director of Sales, I was the sole representative for Calgary, I was responsible for developing new business through consistent cold calling efforts, networking and targeted creative marketing strategies.

Key Successes:

- Ranked in the top 10% in Canada out of 100 Reps.
- Delivered 150% over annual plan.
- Secured 52 new clients in 12 months.

WOW. WOW. WOW.

And, how powerful will your resume look once you add your key successes with #'s and %'s in each and every role?

I'd be tripping over myself to call you before another company scoops you up!

Remember. SHINY gets ATTENTION.

HEY! Something cool just happened!

Do you know what it is?

You just made it through the tough part!

VOILA!!

You have a SHINY new resume that's *going to get results.*

And, this hard work is going to pay off BIG time, because you've now done most of the work needed to **nail the interview. (More on that coming up!)**

I'm so proud of you.

I may even have a tear in my eye.

CHAPTER 5

Lightning Round of Resume Tips ⚡

You've done all the hard work to make your resume shiny – congratulations!

Now we're going to add a few more sparkling ideas to take your resume right to the top 20% of resumes that get past the 11 second skim

Hold on, grab your cup of java and read quickly.

1. Don't Reveal The Private Stuff. EVER.
(and yes, we still see this everyday but we don't want to):

- SIN number
- Marital status
- Date of birth
- Number of children/dependants
- Age (remember back to the recommendations on email addresses – don't use your birth year. You're just telling everyone how old you are. No one needs to know.)
- Medical conditions

Confidential information such as your SIN, marital status, date of birth and number of dependents can only be asked for payroll and benefits administration, once you've been hired.

2. Ditch The Cover Letter.

Cover letters rarely get read.

The only time I'd recommend writing one is if it is specifically requested. Otherwise assume it won't be read. If you put anything good in the letter such as results or your contact details, ensure they also appear on your resume.

3. Grammar Counts.

Spelling mistakes can be a **DEAL BREAKER** on a resume.

People really cringe when I tell them this little fact.

Even *one typo* can have your resume sent straight to the recycle bin.

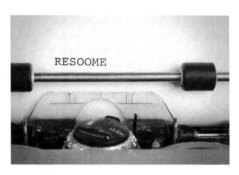

That goes for both the resume as well as an email message.

Take your time. Re-read before sending. Get someone to proof read it for you.

Why is it so important? It shows whether you pay attention to detail or not.

4. Don't talk about yourself in the third person. <u>That's just weird.</u>

5. Think Key-Word Searchable:
Many companies and recruitment firms use their ATS system to rank candidates based on the specific key words for the role.

You'll want to ensure their key words appear in your resume, so you rank higher and get a chance at that first 11 second SKIM.

 The key words will be found in the job posting. Scan the posting for the "must have" requirements and ensure that those words are in your resume. **OK, that might be a sassy tip!**

If you look at most of the TAG postings on our website: www.hideseekfind.com you'll see at the very bottom a note that reads, "Key Words". As much as you're trying to be noticed by employers, we also want you to find us and our job posting. So, we'll dissect the role and use multiple words or phrases that don't appear in our posting as they could be words you're using in your resume.

There are multiple titles that can be used, so if we're looking for an Account Manager, we might also add key words such as: Account Rep, Account Exec, Account Executive, Sales Rep, Territory Rep, Business Development Rep, Business Development Manager, Sales Representative.

It's just another way to ensure that we find each other!

I know. That was a *really* good tip!!

Applying via Email: Don't Make These Critical Mistakes

You've got your shiny new resume in hand and you're **ready to start applying for** *ZIPPY GIGS*.

Imagine all of that work you've done to change your resume from rusty to shiny and then....you do an epic fail?

The EPIC FAIL:

Sending your resume WITHOUT TYPING ONE SINGLE word in the email.

Seriously?

That would be like phoning someone, having your name and number displayed, but not saying a word when the person answers. Just lots of heavy breathing.

You'd never do it. That would be silly. And rude. And weird.

As the person receiving the call, I know it's you phoning, but I have no idea if you're in trouble, want to invite me for wine or you're just calling to say hello.

So, why would you send a blank email with your beautiful shiny resume without at least saying hello?

An email is a PROFESSIONAL piece of communication that's vital when applying for a job.

This is yet another way to stand out and make an impression. Positively or negatively.

A positive impression is made when you show you can construct a proper email, including words! GRIN.

Subject Line: Job Title or Job Number...or both

Email Body: Greeting, message and close

Here's a Shiny example:

> Hello Sheila,
>
> Enclosed please find my resume for your consideration for the Account Executive role.
>
> I am an experienced hunter with 5 years of exceptional results along with a degree in Commerce from the University of Calgary. I was excited to read your posting and feel that I would be a great fit with TAG Recruitment and I am confident that I can exceed all objectives for this role.
>
> I would welcome the opportunity to meet for an interview. I can be reached at 403-234-5678.
>
> Very best,
>
> Amber Wilson

Don't fret about the greeting and closing options. Keep it simple.

Greeting Options:

Dear Sheila
Hello Sheila
Hi Sheila
Sheila,

Closing Options:

Thank you,
Very best,
Best,
Sincerely,
Best regards,
Yours truly,

The greeting and closing in an email can be a little less formal than what's expected in a formal business letter.

The only closing I'm personally not fond of is **"Cheers".**

You're applying for a job - not making a toast over a cocktail.

That's for later...when you get your shiny new *zippy gig*!

And, the last word on email. **Use your own email. Yes, <u>yours.</u>**

It's just **silly** to open an email from Kate Smith only to see a note and resume from Eddy Whyte.

Eddy, my friend, get *your own* email address.

OK, you're probably right. ***That was sassy***. Here it is:

CHAPTER 6

The Big T – Terminations & Other Tough Conversations

Have You Been Canned Like My Mom's Beets?

My mom, Betty, makes the most AMAZING canned pickled beets each fall.

It looks positively dangerous to me with the big canner on the stove filled with boiling water. The result is so worth it. My mom has purple hands, purple tea towels, purple countertops and there's a big reason why.

Canned beets are delectable little morsels. And, Betty loves to make them.

But there's also a canning that isn't so delectable.

Did your stomach just go into a little knot? I'm just going to say it.

You were canned. Terminated. Turfed. Ousted. Fired. #ohshit

The BIG T.

Hey. It happens. For lots of reasons.

I know you feel like crap about it and would love to stuff it under the rug of your resume.

Don't do that.

Why?

Because you *will* be asked about it.

The Big T – 4 Steps to Face the "Were You Fired?" Question

1. **Own it.** Step right into it. What really happened? Before you even think about going to an interview, take some time to work through the Big T.

    Could you have done anything to change the outcome? If so, own that answer. Be accountable.

    After interviewing loads of candidates who have been faced with a Big T – there are ones that simply can't be explained.

    Some examples are:

    A new manager came in and cleaned house...leaving you without a job for no real reason.

    The company was bought/sold and the team was shuffled.

    The role changed and your skills were longer aligning.

    I've got some ideas for you in the next section as well, so don't fret.

2. **Write your answer to the inevitable question** – "Why did you leave XX company?? You'll want to avoid blaming the company and simply explain the scenario very objectively.

3. **Rehearse the answer out loud.** Do you sound positive? Are you explaining the reason? Is it believable?

4. **You're ready for interviewing when you're not dreading answering the Big T question**.

I agree, it's a shitty spot to be in. No sugar coating this one.

Own it. And address the *big pink elephant in the room.*

"All problems become smaller if you don't dodge them but confront them."

— WILLIAM F. HALSEY

There are Really Only 6 Broad Reasons for The Big T:

1. **Performance:** This one is simple. You were brought in to deliver specific results and you didn't. Own it. Know why.

   Was there something going on in your personal life that took away attention from work?

   Did the role change and you were no longer a fit?

   Was there something in the economy that prevented you from delivering?

   Was there a political power play going on in the organization?

   Was it a technical issue? New software, tools, or technology that you couldn't/didn't learn?

   Did you over inflate your skills in the interview? And, then, #ohshit you weren't able to do the job?

2. **Personality** – perhaps you didn't mesh with your colleagues, management or your clients.

   This one happens a lot. I met a very talented fellow who had grown into a VP role over several years. A new CEO came in and simply decided she didn't like him. Over the course of several months, she just made his life difficult and then eventually decided to terminate his employment. It's unfortunate. But it happens.

3. **Values misalignment** – I interviewed a designated accountant who was asked by the owners of the company to "fix" the books. He of course flat out refused as he wasn't going to put his professional reputation or designation on the line. He was asked to leave that day.

   Plain and simple. You were asked to do something that sent your moral compass spinning.

4. **Culture misalignment** – you just didn't fit.

    Rachelle worked as a weight loss consultant. And every now and then she craved a fast food burger, which of course was a big no-no for the lunch room at her place of work. She disguised herself with big sunglasses, zipped through the drive through and then parked blocks away with her seat fully reclined so she wouldn't be spotted as she wolfed down her greasy fries and cheeseburger! Had that taken place daily, likely there would've been a culture misalignment.

5. **Something illegal or unethical happened.** We won't go into this one in detail. We should all have a good pulse on what is right and wrong.

6. **Showing up** – perhaps you just forgot to keep going to work?

True story. It will give you a laugh!

I was speaking to a fellow who failed to show up for training in his first week on the job. The conversation went something like this:

Sheila: David, I just heard from Mary in HR, she said you haven't yet arrived for training this morning. Are you ok?

David: Yeah, my car broke down on the way. I'm just in a cab now.

Sheila: Oh, good, so you'll be at the office in 15 minutes?

David: Ummm, no. I'm going home.

Sheila: Yes, there were two options. Going home or going to work. Unfortunately, you picked the wrong one.

Sheila: David, the very best thing you can do when you get a job, is to go.

That is one of the TAG team's "go to phrases".

And, you guessed it. That was David's last day of work.

"Storms make trees take deeper roots."

— DOLLY PARTON

BIG T terminations happen.

Dust yourself off.

You CAN be a rock star in your next role.

So You Were Laid Off?

Let's clarify something in case you're feeling bad about something you shouldn't be.

Being laid off or going through a down size is a LAY OFF. *It's not a termination.*

Never refer to a lay off or downsize as a **termination**.

Alarm bells go off in my head when I hear the words:

Let-go, Fired or Terminated

Only use those words *if they are in fact true.* And if so, go back to the last section and own your answer as to WHY.

If you were laid off, that's different. It happens. Still shitty, but a different set of circumstances that only requires a brief explanation.

You'll just need to explain **what happened in the *organization*.**

Example:

"The province was in a recession and the company's volumes decreased by 500% in the last quarter."

Give the larger picture.

How many people were laid off? Where you in the first, second or third round of lay-offs? (*Keep in mind: How Big, How Many, How Much?*)

The scope gives me an idea of magnitude. If you were the only person in the entire company of 400 people that was laid off, I'll be digging deeper.

If you were in the last round of lay-offs, and the last person in your department, I'd think you were a keeper.

Gaps in Your Resume: Tough Conversations

After delivering the *Zippy Gig Seminar* recently, a woman approached me after the presentation to ask some advice.

She had a 3 year gap on her resume due to a critical illness. Bless her heart – she wasn't taking it sitting down.

While going through treatment, she enrolled in college to take a full time diploma program in social work. She wanted to be able to counsel others who were undergoing treatment and use both her newfound professional experience with her personal journey.

Let's read that again – **while going through extensive treatment,** she enrolled in a full time diploma program.

Wow. I shared with her what she just told me about herself.

With that comment she told me that *she's resilient.*

She has *incredible drive, determination and grit.*

She's going to *show up each day no matter how she feels.*

She's a *fighter.*

I needed a tissue. We both had tears in our eyes.

I hugged her and said she had *nothing to worry about.*

A future employer would be LUCKY to have her strength.

Most would have been comfortable to rest in bed while going through treatment. She was picking herself up each day and going to school.

Life happens. Curveballs are thrown as they were to this woman.

Gaps can appear when tragic stuff happens.

- Taking care of an ailing parent, family member, spouse or child.
- Having to leave the country to attend to estates.
- Personal illness.
- Out of work/not able to find work.

Be ready to talk about it.

And like the incredibly resilient woman, **think about all of the amazing things you're telling me about how you've handled the curveball.**

Own it all. It will feel good.

"One of the secrets of life is to make stepping stones out of stumbling blocks."
— JACK PENN

CHAPTER 7
Prepare To Ace The Interview

I started running a few years ago when I moved into the city.

A beautiful park is close by and the running paths along the Bow River are just a few kilometres away. When I started running, it was just purely for cardio and general exercise.

I had *no intentions* of running in an actual race....

...until a very cute guy was involved.

He texted on a Friday night to casually say,

"Hey, let's run a 10K race on Sunday morning."

OMG – I panicked.

I ran regularly, but seriously 10K? I'd never run 10K before.

And, I only had a day and a half to get ready to run. Well, I thought, *why the heck not?*

I was nervous as hell.

The race went just fine.

Even though I ran off course - not once, but twice. And, in my true personality, I also convinced other people to come with me. Yes, I sure did.

I finished the race in one piece, with a fairly respectable time considering my silly detours.

And, the best part was the handsome man jumping up and down to hug me at the finish line. GRIN.

I did another 10K a few months later, and I started to dabble thoughts about running a half marathon.

After dinner one January night, my pal Cyndi gave me her training schedule for an April race. I taped it to the inside of my pantry and then just started to train. I ended up injured right before that race, which happens when you're a 40 something training for your first half marathon.

So I chose a new goal. The Calgary Half Marathon.

And, even better is that the TAG Recruitment Gang *all* ran the race. We celebrated on a sunny patio with Caesars and Eggs Bennies post race! I was proud of my team, but thrilled to bits that I finished the race with a reasonably good time and injury free

Training to run 21.1K takes time and commitment.

Quite like creating a shiny resume and preparing for an interview.

The thought of running straight for a couple of hours seemed insane. But I did it... with lots of effort.

I'd dial in my ipod with some **get-your-ass-in-gear music** and I'd say to myself,

Just get started - put one foot in front of the other and just get going.

My legs and lungs were fine for a 2.5 hour training run.

But my HEAD was the problem.

#selfie

I had silly thoughts.

Random illogical thoughts.

You know the little-bit-of-crazy that creeps in when you're doing something for the first time?

> I can't possibly run 21.1K.
> Why do I need to do this?
> My legs will give out.
> Good lord, I could have a heart attack.
> I can't feel my heart beating.
> Why am I wearing an orange tank top and a purple jacket?
> My toes are numb.
> I am going to run out of water.
> Why did I drink so much water?
> I have to pee and I have 5K left.
> I think my hamstrings are seizing.
> OMG my ass is seizing.
> Am I passing out?
> Those geese look mean.
> That goose could take me down.
> OMG the goose is chasing me.
> I'm almost done.
> I should run a full marathon.
> I run like the wind.
> Yay, I'm done!
> I feel GREAT. OK, my feet hurt. And my legs. And hips.
> But this was sooooo worth it.

What CRAZY is in your head about Interviewing?

Probably lots of the same thoughts I had about running.

The list looks surprisingly similar...ok, *except the part about the geese.*

I can't possibly get that job.
Why do I need a new job?
I don't have the skills for that job.
Interviewing is painful.
I could have a heart attack *(I'm sure this has never happened)*
Why did I wear this suit? I should have worn the black suit.
My hands are sweating.
My mouth is dry.
I have to pee.
My legs could give out.
I could pass out.
The hiring manager looks mean.
She's going to ask tough questions.
This is uncomfortable.
Oh gawd, we're starting.
OK, this isn't so bad.
Yay, I aced the interview!
I'm sooooo getting an offer.
I love interviewing. I'm a star!

Isn't it strange how we have these *crazy* random thoughts?

Sassy Sheila Advice: Get your head into a different space. Know this:

99% of the hiring managers you meet – WANT to find every reason to HIRE you. You just have to help them to be right.

Most hiring managers want to get back to their regular work and stop interviewing. Most aren't interested in interviewing for sport. They need to fill the position.

They've seen your resume. You've had a phone chat. And, now you're in the hot seat.

They've liked what they've read on your shiny resume. And, they liked what you said on the phone to invite you for an interview.

Heads Up.
The casual phone chat isn't so casual.

One quick point before we dive into the interview process – let's talk about that casual phone chat. Here's the truth – *it's not a casual phone chat*. It's a mini interview.

Before both of us want to invest an hour of our time for a formal interview, we want to ensure that the role in question could be a good fit.

In the 5 minute conversation I'm assessing:

- Your phone manner – energy, enthusiasm, interest level, grammar and overall communication skills.

- I will be very bold and also ask you your current and future target income. Yes, that might seem direct, but I want to ensure we're in the same range. It wouldn't be fair to ask you to spend an hour in an interview with me if the salary wasn't even close to where you were hoping to be.

- I'll certainly tell you a bit more about the role and who the role is with (if working with an agency recruiter – we want to ensure you haven't applied for the role already). I'm gauging if this really is the type of role that will have you hopping out of the bed in the morning.

- Do you have the skills and background (at a high level) to be a solid candidate for the role.

- If I have a deadline for the role, does our timing work?

If you are a "yes" to the above, chances are you'll be invited for an interview.

Sidebar funny story: After doing a routine pre-screen interview with a candidate, I invited him for an interview and confirmed the necessary details on when and where. He was booked. He passed the mini interview. Thennnnnnn, he kept talking. He said, "Wow, I'm soooo surprised you asked me for an interview!! I thought I totally screwed up that earlier question." Once you're invited for the interview, ensure that you don't talk yourself out of the invitation.

You've got every chance to ace the interview and get the *Zippy Gig*.

2 BIG "Must-do's" To Prepare For Your Interview:

The worst thing you can do is walk into an interview and just "wing it". Yes, you're going to prepare.

An interview really is a sales presentation on **YOU**.

Think back to those dreaded public speaking moments in high school. If you're like me, I was terrified.

Chances are you stood nervously gripping cue cards and rehearsed your speech out loud. Of course you did.

Think of your interview as an on-stage performance. You need to rehearse what you're going to say.

1. Rehearse out loud.

Why?

Here's the cool thing.

When you rehearse out loud - what you're saying is committed to short term memory. If a case of the nerves hit, your short term memory kicks in and you can recall what you've rehearsed.

It's a cool brain thing.

Here's the not-so-cool-thing.

If you haven't rehearsed out loud, everything on your resume is resting in your long term memory.

And, if those nerves hit (let's say you were expecting 1 person in the interview and you walk into a panel of 5 people) your long term memory is shot.

You get all flustered. All of a sudden you can't remember what role you were in 5 years ago. Hell – you can't even remember your name. And, the interview is blown.

If you say,

"Can I see my resume, so I can remember?".

Your interview is now done. Cooked. Oh-so-over.

You've just told me that you don't have a memory.

You can't even remember your background?

That's not a good thing.

2. Know your career history off the top of your head.

I've said to many a nervous candidate,

"You're not convincing me that you even know your own background."

Why? They're fumbling around, getting mixed up – it's like they're trying to convince me they are someone else (and doing a very bad job I might add).

So here's an easy rule. Plan what you're going to say in advance.

You might be saying, "Yeah, that's great, but I still have no idea what to say!"

Not to worry, those answers are coming up.

Before we dive into the *"what to say"*, I was thrilled to interview some experts at being "on stage".

How do Experts Prepare for their On-Stage Performance?

I was thrilled to connect with an old college friend, who is one of the most natural, funny and talented musicians I know.

My pal, **Tim Tamashiro, Drinky jazz singer & radio host**. He's recorded 6 jazz albums and is an incredibly talented and engaging performer.

I think you can learn a few things from him for your next interview.

Here's my chat with Tim:

Sheila: How do you prepare to deliver a flawless stage performance? (Yes, they appear flawless.)

Tim: I don't ever want to deliver a flawless show. I always want to do an entertaining show. Mistakes can be extremely entertaining. Mistakes happen in life and on stage. I'm prepared to deal with anything that comes up on stage by just being human.

Always laugh at yourself on stage. Show humility. The audience will always be on your side if you just show them that you're just like them. It's a good thing to be vulnerable. You don't ever have to be perfect on stage or anytime in life.

Tim Tamashiro, Drinky jazz singer & radio host. *(Photo courtesy of Tim Tamashiro)*

Being on stage is just like being a gracious host in your home. Help everyone feel comfortable and encourage them to enjoy themselves.

Sheila: What are your top tips for being prepared?

Tim: My top tip for being prepared for the stage comes from way back in the vaudeville days. Always have "insurance" material that you know works every time. You're going to be judged based on your overall performance. Find two or three things that work every time and have them in your back pocket in case you need them.

Choose topics that are recognizable, understandable and emotional. Tell great stories with a nice variety of emotions (and laughs). Tell them over and over again. They are insurance for you and the audience.

Sheila: What happens if you FLUB?

Tim: This might be weird but I actually look forward to making mistakes on stage. I'm most comfortable AFTER I make my first mistake each gig. It's like the audience has just seen you fall on your face. They're all eager to see you get back up again. When you pick yourself up and redeem yourself, they feel just as relieved as you do.

If you flub you flub. Laugh at yourself and move on. Let the audience know you flubbed too. Try one more time to get your flub right. I promise they'll wait for you and support you. The audience sees themselves in you and they want you to succeed.

Sheila: How do you keep nerves under control?

Tim: Nerves are a natural part of being in front of people. In the past, I didn't think I got nervous at all before I went on stage. I found that I would often yawn before I went on stage. *Turns out that yawning is a coping mechanism for dealing with stress.*

In the past few years I do find myself getting anxious before taking the stage. To re-lax I use a cool technique I read about recently in a study. I imagine myself smelling a **brand new box of Crayola Crayons**. According to the study, just imagining the smell of a fresh box of Crayolas can reduce blood pressure by as much as 10 points. I've tried it and I feel quite chilled out as I stroll on to stage.

Awesome insight Tim – thank you! Great advice – be able to laugh at yourself, roll with flubs, show humility, be yourself and tell great stories. And, we'll all be zipping out to buy a brand new box of Crayolas. Who doesn't remember the excitement of a new box of crayons?

I was delighted to reach out to **Cory Woron** who has the coolest gig out there – he's a Commentator for **SportsCentre** and **TSN**. I thought he would have some incredible insight in preparing for interviews and being on camera.

Sheila: When sitting in front of high profile athletes or any of the greats - What do you do to prepare for those interviews?

Cory Woron, Commentator SportsCentre and TSN. (Photo courtesy of TSN.)

Cory: I remember the first time Wayne Gretzky called me by name, I thought, *WOW he knows who I am.*

That left an impression on me. So whenever I know I am going to get an interview with someone I want to try and connect on a personal level. Anyone can talk about stats or accomplishments and certainly that will be a part of the conversation. But I do my homework to find out if they have any personal ties to the place or the event where I might be talking to them. They may have a story in their past that might help others see what kind of a person they are. For instance, I was interviewing golfer JB Holmes at a sponsor's event prior to the Canadian Open. JB had brain surgery 4 years ago for a Chiari malformation. We talked about that time in his life - what it meant for his livelihood, the struggles he was going through prior and how his health is now. He was also on his high school golf team in grade 3. I wanted to know how that would even happen and it led to a lot of great stories. Our audience loved that we could weave personal stories into our talk, which gave them a much better understanding for JB as a person, and someone to cheer for, not just a golfer.

But you have to do your homework and be prepared. You also have to be an active listener, because sometimes the follow up question leads to an even more interesting place.

Sheila: You're well accustomed to being "on stage" in front of the camera – what do you do to keep nerves in check?

Cory: I don't get nervous much anymore. Some events are obviously bigger than others and the adrenaline flows a bit more. But I think if you are prepared and confident in your ability it's easy to use that energy in a positive manner and it helps you to deliver a great show. Experience has taught me that nervous energy is great energy. It's nothing to be afraid of. Staying focused on the task at hand is a must.

Sheila: What would be your best advice in handling the unexpected curveballs of being on live television?

It's funny because stuff is always happening. Most of the time it's all little stuff and no one in the audience would ever know. An item didn't get edited in time, so it gets dropped last second - a computer freezes in the control room so our graphics and scoreboards are unavailable for awhile - to having our set collapse on me, that was actually a big one. It was while we were in a piece of tape so it didn't get caught on camera, thankfully. I was mildly concussed, but managed to get my wits in order to finish the show. I guess it's the old mantra – the show must go on.

The most important aspect is to just keep composed, so you can think clearly and quickly. Our producers and directors are all world class, and they are on the ball as well. As a group we all react and move on as best as we can and when it's an obvious technical problem, I think the audience is more forgiving of the hiccup. Having a short memory is good in these instances. It's easy to dwell on mistakes, but really there is nothing you can do once they are committed and you move on.

GREAT advice from a pro. Be prepared. Do your research. Listen. Ask great questions.

And, chances are you won't have a set collapse on your head in the middle of an interview.

I'd be over the moon if Wayne Gretzky addressed me by name too!

4 Ways Your Most Critical Interview Question Will Be Asked:

Most candidates would rather go to the dentist for a root canal than go to an interview.

I'm going to change your mind on this one, sunshine.

You're going to *love interviewing* once you know what to expect.

So Where Does Interview Anxiety Come From?

The anxiety for most candidates comes when they realize they're going to have to highlight virtually everything on their resume.

And, if you didn't create a shiny resume, it's terrifying to think about how the heck you're going to talk about the bullets.

But, you're super smart. And, you've created a SHINY resume. So, this part is going to be **EASY** for you.

Pssst.

Here's A *Shiny Sneaky Secret.*

Hiring managers and recruiters all really ask the SAME question. They just ask it differently. (*Sneaky cats*)

The 4 Variations of THE question that *will* be asked....every time:

1. Bring your resume to life for me.

2. Tell me about your current position.

3. Tell me about your previous position.

4. Walk me through your background.

This is where the *out of body experience* starts for most people.

Sheer fear of what the heck to talk about.

So, it starts.

The *meandering* ramble.

You can feel your mouth moving but your brain sure isn't firing.

It's as painful for the interviewer to listen to as it is for you to deliver.

But it doesn't have to be like this.

GUESS WHAT?

If you've done a SHINY resume you've already got a gold star because you can answer this MASTER question with ease.

You already have a few very concise sentences from the STEP 1 preparation of your resume, so bringing your resume to life in the interview will be EASY!

Time yourself.

If you can rattle through your resume in less than 5 minutes, that's waaaay too short. And, you're missing the important stuff.

If you're still spewing out words at the 45 minute mark, the interviewer deserves a gold medal for not throwing their pen at you. Kidding.

The magic amount of time is 15 minutes. OK, 10 if you're new to your career.

15 minutes is ample time to SUCCINCTLY walk through your career history.

You'll just need to rehearse those sentences out loud and you'll nail the BIG interview question – no matter how they throw it at you.

5 things The Interviewer Wants To Learn About Each Role:

Most candidates I work with tell me they have absolutely *no idea* what to say in an interview.

Once I start the interview, yup, **the deer-in-the-headlights** look appears on their face.

Let me unravel the mystery.

5 things we're looking to learn from you:

1. What was the role and what were you accountable for?

2. What level did you report to?

3. How many people did the same role?

4. How successful were you – yes, the *sexy numbers*.

5. Why did you leave or why are you looking to leave?

Look familiar? Of course it does. GRIN.

It's the SHINY resume formula.

Those Dreaded *"Tell me about a Time"* Questions:

Yes, they're *dreaded* by virtually every candidate that I've met.

The "tell me about a time" questions are called **behavioural based questions**.

The reason they're asked is simple.

Past performance and behaviours are the best indicators of your future performance.

When creating Step 2 – the sexy results on your resume, I shared that a hiring manager is *hiring your previous results.*

Because if you've been successful in each of your last positions, chances are you'll *continue to be successful.*

Behavioural based questions allow a bit more of a dive into you at your best and also at your worst.

A hiring manager needs to know what to expect on both your best and worst days.

"Sometimes the questions are complicated and the answers are simple."

— Dr. Seuss

6 Behavioural-based Questions To Prepare For:

Tell me about a time...

1. When you went above and beyond? What was the result?

2. You had a conflict with a co-worker. What happened and how was it resolved?

3. When you brought a new idea to your manager. Was it implemented? Why or why not?

4. When you disagreed with a decision made by your manager?

5. You were recognized for outstanding work?

6. When you missed your performance targets. How did you get back on track?

The key to getting through these questions is to PREPARE. Take some time to think about examples to each of the questions above.

We want to hear the specific scenario and how you handled it.

It shows us more of who you are, your personality, how you handle difficult situations as well as how you create success.

Feeling the pressure?

You won't if you take the time to prepare.

10 Additional Questions to Prepare For:

 Sassy Sheila speaking here... I think the dumbest question still asked is:
1. Tell me about your strengths and weaknesses.

The answers are always the same, which is why I don't ask the question. But, lots of people still ask that silly question, so prepare for it.

Be a stand out with *clever* responses.

And I do mean clever.

Don't use these old worn out **RUSTY** responses that we've all heard over and over again.

My Strengths: I'm a team player. I love what I do. I'm really good at my job.

My Weaknesses: I take on too much. I care too much. I'm a perfectionist. I work too much.

BORING. OVER-USED. DULL. YAWN.

You're going to bring your *clever* and *shiny self!*

My Strengths – simply tie to your shiny results and how you've been able to achieve them.

My Weaknesses – think about where you're stretching your performance to get to the next level in your career.

2. Where do you want to be professionally in the next 3 – 5 years?

If you've created a shiny resume, your target position will be very clear. Think about where you'd like to be in the position after this next one.

3. Tell me what you know about our company.

Research the company. You should know what the company does, a bit of history (when it was started), geographical locations, awards and perhaps who the executive team are, and what the company does of course.

4. What's your ideal job?

A job interview isn't the time to be *wishy- washy*. Give some thought to what your ideal job is. **HINT** – ideally it's the one you're interviewing for.

5. Tell me something about your background that I wouldn't know by reading your resume. (This is an opportunity to highlight a cool "interest").

I LOVE this question. If you've unearthed something really interesting for your "interests" section, this is the place to spotlight it.

6. What do you really like about your present job?

What's the juiciest part of your current gig? If you could amplify the great parts of your role, what are they?

7. What would you change about your present job?

We all have parts of our job that aren't our favourite. What are they for you? Keep it positive though.

8. Tell me about your biggest success or career milestone.

Pull one of your Step 2 Key Successes from your resume. (See, all of that work on creating a shiny resume is paying off BIG time.)

9. What was your biggest achievement in your last role?

GRIN. Yes, it's all on your SHINY resume.

10. Is there anything else you were hoping to cover?

I always end with this question – I want to ensure I haven't missed anything.

Write out your answers to these questions. Rehearse out loud. Own the answers. You're well on your way to ACING the interview.

But, wait! There's more. I've asked some top Canadian executives for their insight on favourite interview questions and what makes a candidate a stand-out.

Read the next page to learn 14 insightful interview questions!

14 BONUS Questions From Some Smart Cookies:

I reached out to some really smart senior business leaders to ask for their favourite interview question. Yes – this is incredible insider stuff!

"I love asking, 'Tell me about the last book you read, and what you thought of it.' It's a nice natural question with no correct answer. It might be unexpected, though, so it gives me a good sense of how well the candidate can respond on their feet."

Todd Hirsch, Chief Economist
ATB Financial

"What did you want to be when you were in junior high school?" "I think this gives me insight into the journey that got them to where they are now. Did they always want to be in their current profession? Did they have some other aspirations, and if so, what changed? Did they have the presence of mind as a teenager to think about the future and their place in it?"

James M. Bond, QC, President
Western Life Assurance Co.

"What is the biggest misconception about you and how to manage its existence?"

Mark Breslaw, Vice President, People & Culture
TELUS

"Tell me something in your career that you have done that you are really proud of."

Janice Webster, SVP of HR
Solium Capital

"I like asking managers for examples of when they have developed a direct report to the point where they have surpassed their own level of performance. It helps me look at how humble the person is, whether they can define 'how' they support candidates to truly develop them past their own capabilities. Many times there are examples of how they now report to that person that they helped become a better leader, and that's a big one for me."

Paula Breeze, Vice President, Human Resources,
Aveda Transportation & Energy Services

"What advice would you give someone going into a leadership position for the first time?"

Paul Trudel, National Director, HR & Professional Development
PCL Construction

"Why should I hire you? What makes you the best candidate?"

And:

"Supposing you are hired: one year from now, you wake up thinking, 'This has been the best work decision I've made – to accept the job.' What would have taken place in that year for you to feel this way?"

Carol Ionel, Vice President Human Resources
& Team from Houston & Abu Dhabi
Enerflex

"What is the greatest adversity you have ever overcome? Describe what it was in vivid detail and how you overcame it."

And:

Describe these 3 people in 3 words:
   a. Husband/Wife
   b. Best Friend
   c. Mother/Father

People rarely break their behavioural patterns from their internal environment with their external environment. People with great ambition tend to invest their time with others who have great ambition if they are synchronized with their purpose. This is a great screening tool on many levels."

Frank Lonardelli, President & CEO
Arlington Street Investments

"What is your proudest accomplishment in life and in work?"

Mark Smye, Vice President Sales
De Lage Landen

"Picture yourself successful in getting this role and it's now a year down the road. What have you accomplished? How did you approach your first year?"

Dion Kostiuk, Vice President, Human Resources
Keyera Corp.

"I really enjoy it when a candidate asks why the position is vacant. The challenge for the interviewer is to be able to explain without violating privacy and keeping a positive spin."

Sue Wood, HR Advisor, AB, SK, MB
Yellow Pages

"If I were to say to a bunch of people who know you, 'Give me three adjectives that best describe you', what would they say?"

Shelley Vandenberg, President
First Calgary Financial

Aren't these questions amazing?

And thought provoking?

And aren't you glad you experienced them here FIRST vs. on your interview?

Let's give the tables a big spin and now YOU get to ask some questions too.

7 Smart Questions to Ask On An Interview

You've made it through the interview. It went really well. Yay!!

Then that last question comes where the tables turn. The interviewer smiles, and says…

What questions can I answer for you?

POOF!

The Deer In Headlights Is Back!

Don't be a dumb ass and NOT any ask questions.
Or worse yet, asking silly questions.

If you don't ask *ANY* questions you look terrified and ill-prepared.

Not the best look for you.

Silly **questions are:**

1. What's the salary?
2. What are the benefits?
3. How many weeks vacation?
4. When can I take my first vacation days?
5. Are sick days covered?
6. Do you close during the holiday season?
7. Is there a bonus?
8. Are salary increases given each year?

You get the point.

These are all about YOU. And, if you're more concerned about how much time you get to spend away from your job, I will likely be *de-selecting* you as fast as you've uttered these dumb questions.

I want you to up your game.

It's Time to Tap into your Clever, Curious Mind Here.

Ask questions to once again STAND out, you shiny thing!
Some ideas are:

1. Why do you love working here?

2. Why is the role vacant?

3. What are the top skills and experience you're looking for in the ideal candidate?

4. If successful, what would training look like?

5. What would a career look like with the organization?

6. What do you see as the biggest challenge for this role?

7. Do you see any skill gaps in what you're looking for in the ideal candidate and my background?

8. Would there be any reason I wouldn't be invited for a second interview?

You don't have to memorize the questions. Have them pre-written and take them with you.

If the hiring manager hasn't outlined, DO ask what the next steps and timing will be.

We asked our Smart Cookies for their perspective:

Sheila Question: What is the very best end-of-interview question you've ever been asked by a candidate?

They were thrilled to share some very clever candidate questions:

"Why do you do what you do? If candidates asked this at the beginning of the interview, it would be far 'more clever.'"

Frank Lonardelli, President & CEO
Arlington Street Investments

"What would prevent you from hiring me today?"

Shelley Vandenberg, President
First Calgary Financial

"I'm not sure that it was necessarily clever, but one gal asked me, 'Where do you buy your shoes? They're fantastic!' The question was perhaps a bit of blatant flattery, but it also showed a bit of attention to details of things around her. But you can't get away with the shoe comment with EVERYONE. The shoes really DO need to be fantastic, otherwise you'll come across as insincere. Find something really noteworthy about the person, the artwork in the room, the view out the window....SOMETHING! And comment on that."

Todd Hirsch, Chief Economist,
ATB Financial

"What would you be doing if you weren't a lawyer? I like this question because it shows that the candidate is at least feigning interest in your career and considering what got you to where you are now. (In short, it's flattering.)"

James M. Bond, QC, President
Western Life Assurance Co.

"When do I start?"

Dion Kostiuk, Vice President, Human Resources
Keyera Corp.

"How do you define integrity?"

Sue Wood, HR Advisor, AB, SK, MB
Yellow Pages

"How will the company make me feel welcome?" (I stumbled through that answer a little bit. ☺)

And:

"In order for me not to lose money for the company, will I be given an introduction about the company? What sort of training do you offer?"

Carol Ionel, Vice President, Human Resources
And Team from Houston & Abi Dhabi
Enerflex

"Candidates who try to close/qualify the interview/opportunity."

Mark Smye, Vice President, Sales
De Lage Landen

You'll be a knock out with clever questions!

You should be feeling *very confident* about your next interview.

I hope you've had a bit of an **Ah Ha** while reading this chapter.

The reason your previous interviews were **flat-lining disasters** is because your resume wasn't helping you. Your rusty old resume caused you to be a *meandering mess* in your interview.

Spurting out words, disjointed ideas, and rambling.

BUT, because you're a **smarty pants** and you followed the easy 2-step formula on how to write a shiny resume, you now know SUCCINCTLY how to describe your role and key successes.

You can answer KEY critical questions to bring your resume to life with EASE. You should now welcome the opportunity to highlight those two or three pages and ACE your next interview.

Your FEAR about interviews should be gone. You'll ace the interview and get the *Zippy Gig!*

Congratulations!!

Because you put in the effort to create a SHINY resume – you likely breezed through this chapter.

A FUN reward for you - A bonus Chapter on all of the little "lightning" things that'll give you a jolt, and keep you on track to get the *Zippy Gig.*

CHAPTER 8
Smoking Hot Lightning Interview Tips ⚡

1. **Learn to extend a firm handshake.** No limp fish here. But don't be a bone-crusher either.

2. **Leave the java in the car.** Bringing a giant *Timmies* coffee just looks a bit too casual.

3. **Bring a copy of your resume.** Stuff happens. Maybe my printer just blew up or perhaps I can't access my computer. (Weird stuff happens.) So, just be prepared and bring a copy. It is also a good idea to have it in front of you for reference during the interview.

 Sassy Sheila note: Never reach across the table to take the interviewer's copy. They've been writing private notes and questions throughout. They aren't meant to be shared.

4. **Bring a copy of your references.** You'll need 2 – 3 professional references. They must be former direct supervisors or managers who can provide an objective evaluation of your work.

   Your aunt, best friend, cousin or favourite uncle will of course only have glowing things to say about you. They aren't considered professional references and shouldn't be used. Sorry. I know they adore you. They can gush about you on Facebook.

5. **Listen to the question and answer *that* specific question.** Yes, it happens. Nerves hit and the candidate answers a completely unrelated question. If you hear the same question being asked, it is simply because you missed answering the question we asked. **We're giving you a second shot.**

6. **Arrive no more than 10 minutes early**. Arriving earlier than 15 minutes is just poor planning. If you arrive 30, 45 or an hour early, it is poor planning. Find a coffee shop in the building or down the street to burn up some of the extra time. Kudos to you for not being late!

7. **Turn off your cell phone**. Worse yet, if it rings, don't answer it! Yes, that has happened. A lot.

8. **Know what job you've applied for and how your experience relates.**

9. **Body language.** Just like mom said, "sit up straight." Make eye contact (not to the point of being creepy). Don't cross your arms. No eye rolling. No slouching.

10. **Smile.** Look interested and happy to be in the interview chair.

11. **Have quick access to a pen.** It should be clipped to your folder or portfolio. Not at the bottom of your cavernous purse.

12. **Take off your overcoat and stay awhile.** If you leave your coat and scarf on, it looks like you're about to dash the minute things get tough.

13. **If a business card is given – take it.** It's just poor manners to leave it on the table.

14. **Breathe.** The interviewer wants to find every reason to hire you. Just help them to be right.

15. **Make eye contact.** Smile with your eyes. Yes, try it. It works.

16. **Be excited to be at the interview.** Many a candidate has blown it simply because they gave off an air of disinterest. Be interested.

17. **Have energy and enthusiasm in your voice.**

18. A nice portfolio or even a file folder will work to hold your documents: resume, references, details about the company, position posting and other documents.

19. Laptops, tablets or iPads can work well, as long as they don't take up a huge amount of time to open. I've interviewed many candidates who spent most of their time looking at their screen and they forgot to look up to make eye contact.

20. If you're in a design profession and need to show your portfolio, of course you're the exception. (But you'd still have it prepared and ready) For the rest – yes a paper resume can work much better!

21. **If you think to yourself, "gosh, I've been talking for a looooonnnnggg time."** It has been. Stop talking. Re-group. If you feel that you've meandered off topic. Say it. Grin.

22. Always go solo to an interview. This isn't an event to take children, friends, parent or spouse. (As I write this, a woman brought her husband to her interview. Worse yet, he had a case of the "ah-hems" and a serious nasal issue. I would have left my office to offer a tissue, but I needed to keep writing.)

23. Research the person who will be interviewing you. LinkedIn is an easy go-to. I always appreciate a candidate who's taken the time to research my background and TAG. (More on being a stand-out in Chapter 11.)

24. Let your personality shine through.

25. When you are interviewing with an agency recruiter it *is an actual interview.* We hear all of the time, "Oh, I'd never say that in a 'real' interview. I'm just telling you." Oh, the stuff we've heard!

26. There are loads of very snazzy words to use to make a point besides swearing. Although we all chuckled at the lovely candidate who in an interview with Rachelle, leaned in with a hushed voice and said, "Could I curse when I tell you this story?" GRIN. While I can't tell you the story, it sure made us laugh!

How To Keep Your Nervous Face Under Wraps

I've had the pleasure of working with a very talented photographer, Kirstey Ball, Owner of SuperCorporate People. She's the talent behind my photo on the cover.

Having done several shoots with Kirstey over the years, she is a master at helping to keep my "nervous face" from creeping to the surface in photos.

I'm not sure what the heck happens when I see that camera, but my go-to is a fairly frozen, panicked, nervous face and I'm sure my eyes just look pinched. It was a natural to reach out to Kirstey when writing this section to gain her professional insights.

Sheila: How do you get people to look so natural? And, keep nervous face at bay?

Kirstey: Nervousness comes from fear. Fear comes from the unknown. It's totally rational to be nervous, in an interview process there are a lot of unknowns. However, there is one incredibly powerful weapon you have that trumps everything from the minute you make contact with the interviewer and can help influence how they connect with you.

Your image and persona.

I'm not talking about how good looking you are, or how intelligent you are. I'm talking about how you project yourself, how infectious you are, how you make the most of what you have and how you just somehow seem to make everything about you look and feel so amazing. This is confidence. This comes from knowing yourself so well (good and bad) that there can't possibly be any fear present. You are your best version of 'you' and therefore there just cannot be any competition. You are the only 'you' and you are the best one there is!

As a fashion and corporate photographer I have to get my clients to ooze this confidence within minutes of meeting them for a shoot and sometimes only having ten minutes to capture that and have them LOVE their picture!

Kirstey shared some fun images and pointers of herself to demonstrate.

MIRROR/CAMERA REALITY CHECK

These are the things I hate about myself. Whenever I'm about to see photos of myself, I have abject horror and paranoia that this is what I will see. I am my worst judge. Focusing on this does NOT create confidence!

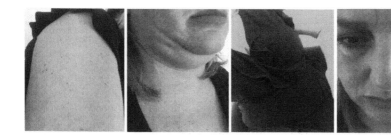

Focusing on making the most of myself using posture and knowing my best angles, enables me to highlight my best features and portrays me as a confident and attractive person.

Standing or sitting square on can look timid, intimidating, awkward or nervous and uncomfortable. Definitely not warm and friendly. No genuine smile.

Granted, this is more of a photographic pose, but look at the difference a genuine smile makes, the hand on the hip could just as easily be held out for a hand shake, and the learning forwards at an angle creates genuine interest.

Sitting at a slight angle, leaning forwards with strong eye contact and a soft smile shows interest while listening, arms show relaxed openness and connection.

We asked our Smart Cookies for their perspective.

Sheila Question: What are the top 1 or 2 things that make a candidate a stand out for you?

"Self confidence without ego, some knowledge of my company and a genuine smile."

James M. Bond, QC, President
Western Life Assurance Co.

"Comfortable and authentic. Not cocky, just knows themselves well."

Dion Kostiuk, Vice President Human Resources
Keyera Corp.

"The kinds of things that demonstrate the candidate is a well rounded individual. I had one candidate with a great GPA and lots of experience in hockey (playing, coaching, etc.). So I thought, "OK, you're a smart jock. You're a dime-a-dozen." But then at the VERY end of the resume he had: Grade 10 Royal Conservatory of Music (Piano). A smart hockey player who is also an accomplished pianist? Now that IS surprising!"

Todd Hirsch, Chief Economist
ATB Financial

"They look me in the eye when answering questions. (I dislike the wandering eye, or they look at their feet when they answer questions.)"

And:

"They demonstrate that they've done their homework on our credit union. One of the main questions we ask is "What do you know about our credit union?" If they cannot answer the question or stumble with vague generalities, I know they have not taken the time to read our website, Google news articles, or learn about the credit union industry."

Shelley Vandenberg, President
First Calgary Financial

"Confidence – including preparation, attire, strength of character.
Cleanliness of their car – it says a lot about their character.
The "stand out" for me would be a confident, groomed, prepared individual driving a well taken care of vehicle!"

Darin Wyatt, General Manager
Rotork Controls Canada

"Great energy. Well spoken. Evidence that they've done their homework and research."
Mark Smye, Vice President Sales
De Lage Landen

"In general terms, people fall into two categories; they are either Aspirational or Inspirational.

My experience with "aspirational" people is:

A.   They have massive ambition
B.   They possess a strong locus of control
C.   If placed in an ambitious environment, they will both propel and excel past the current experience. THEY WANT AND NEED MORE.

Inspirational individuals tend to require a significant amount of external reinforcement to maintain their motivation. Their three characteristics are:

A.   They require third party validation
B.   They need environmental success to feel valuable
C.   They have a pleasant demeanor, but a low locus of control."

Frank Lonardelli, President & CEO
Arlington Street Investments

"Something as simple as good manners goes a long way. This can include a follow up thank you (email is fine, although I have received a few hand written notes in the past). *(We agree Sue! So much that we dedicated an entire chapter to follow up.)* Also speaking professionally, making eye contact and engaging in conversation during the interview.   Preparation in finding out about the company, position, industry and bringing questions that reflect that preparation."

Sue Wood, HR Advisor
Yellow Pages, AB, SK, MB

"Enthusiasm and good questions."

"Doing preliminary research about the company, industry trends, showing preparation and forethought at the interview. Post interview follow up messages – either in the form of email, written note or a call depending on the circumstances."

Carol Ionel, *Vice President Human Resources*
Houston & Abu Dhabi Teams
Enerflex

Sheila Question: What would you like to see more often from candidates?

"Preparation – by doing some preparation an applicant will feel more in control and will appear cool, calm and collected as a result. Those are all qualities that I look for in a candidate. I am always surprised that applicants don't take the time to conduct simple research on the company history, recent financial statements, recent news stories, learning who the key players are, learning more about the company culture and values and learn more about the products and services we offer.

I would like to see more applicants send thank you notes or thank you emails after an interview. Most applicants don't bother to do it. Sending a thank you note – if done reasonably well – will definitely not hurt your chances at a job. More often, it will improve the impression you left after the interview, making you stand out from your competitors."

Shelley Vandenberg, President
First Calgary Financial

"Better research on the company. Often they don't learn enough about the company, so it comes across as just wanting the job. Just be yourself. Don't try to be something that you're not."

Dion Kostiuk, *Vice Present Human Resources*
Keyera Corp.

"I think that there is a lot of unnecessary focus on the grade point average in school. Maybe we've all been conditioned this way, but I'm more interested in someone with a 3.0 GPA and lots of interesting volunteer experience in things OUTSIDE their major, than someone with a perfect 4.0 GPA and nothing else interesting. So for me, I look for the well-rounded person, not the smartest one in the classroom."

Todd Hirsch, Chief Economist
ATB Financial

"Preparation. More questions about the company and the environment. Questions about potential growth."

Carol Ionel, Vice President Human Resources &
Houston Team
Enerflex

"Our entire company is based on hiring individuals that not only possess "gold medal resumes" (which I would consider table stakes) but also people who can not stand to lose. I fundamentally believe that the flaw in hiring has always been trying to find "the winners". Instead we look for people who cannot stand to lose. With this perspective, winning becomes a foregone conclusion and the goal becomes mitigating all risk to ensure you never lose."

Vince Lombardi said it best, "the quality of a person's life is in direct relation to their commitment to excellence regardless of their chosen field of endeavour."

Frank Lonardelli, President & CEO
Arlington Street Investments

Wow. You've heard it from some top executives on things that make candidates become stand outs.

You probably noticed some common themes too!

- Confidence & authenticity
- Smile, positivity, energy & enthusiasm
- Eye contact
- Good manners & follow up
- Grooming – dressing sharp
- Research on the company
- Being prepared
- Demonstrating your uniqueness
- Asking great questions

The super good news is that I've got dedicated chapters for you on these topics just up ahead!

Chapter 9 is all about Dressing Sharp.

Chapter 11 will show you how to follow up to be a stand out.

If you've done your homework in creating a shiny resume with sexy results, you'll exude confidence and be beaming. We've already covered examples of great questions, so you are set!

"The only place where success comes before work is in the dictionary."

— DONALD KENDALL

CHAPTER 9
Dressing SHARP Gives You An Edge

**"Style is a way to say who you are
without having to speak."**
— RACHEL ZOE

This is a little chapter but BIG on how it can help you get hired.

From the minute you shake hands and say hello to the hiring manager, judgments have already started about your overall image and rightness for the role.

**"It only takes 7 seconds for us to judge
another person when we first meet them."**
— LINDA BLAIR
CLINICAL PSYCHOLOGIST AND
AUTHOR OF STRAIGHT TALKING

7 SECONDS

By the time you get to the hiring manager's office the first 7 seconds have already ticked by and the impressions have started to form.

Let's talk about why being SHARPLY dressed is critical.

Why? It gives you a big competitive edge.

The first 7 seconds are a scan of how you're dressed, cleanliness (clothes, shoes, hair, hands) how you smell, how you shake hands, eye contact and the confidence of the first words spoken.

There was a song waayyyyy back in the 80's by a band called ZZ Top (Google it). They wrote a super catchy song with the lyrics:

"Every girl is crazy about a sharp dressed mannnnn"

A great definition of SHARP is: when you or an object looks very nice.

"After I put on my suit, I thought to myself, "I look so f'ing sharp, I could cut someone"

That sentence made me LAUGH!

It might be a bit extreme, but you'll sure remember it when you do that last glance at yourself in the mirror before heading to your next interview. GRIN

SHARP means you have it TOGETHER and you look like it in every way.

Ironed, pressed, put together, clean, covered (more on this one a bit later). You've put thought into it.

You know who you are and how you want to express yourself.

So How Can You Be Sharp?

You can be sharp in a business suit.

Sharp in jeans and work boots.

Sharp is an attitude.

You're completely put together on the outside and on the inside. Buffed, polished and put together. You're confident and prepared.

Sharp *also* means what your hair, jewelry, shoes, car, phone, purse, bag, nails, laptop, pen, and coffee cup look like. You don't have to spend a mint. You can be very budget friendly and still look put together.

Clean, polished and shone all make you look sharp.

"In our industry wearing jeans to an interview is fine, however, ensure that they are clean, not ripped and that you have a decent shirt on – not one from a Metallica concert. Yes, it's a true story."

Sue Wood, HR Advisor, AB, SK, MB
Yellow Pages

Here's A Stat That Will Make You Shine Your Shoes:

58% of hiring decisions are made on your non verbal cues like attire.

Dress For The Role You're Interviewing For.

Since I was a little kid, I've always wanted to wear a suit and carry a briefcase.

True story.

I recall seeing a magazine cover of a woman wearing a navy suit and carrying a briefcase. It was locked into my 5 year old brain. That was going to be me. As a 5 year old I had no idea what my job or my career was going to be. But, I certainly knew what I'd be wearing.

Dressing well IS dressing SHARP.

If you're interviewing for a corporate position, you should be in a suit. That goes for both men and women. If you know the corporate culture is more relaxed, then ditch the tie.

If you're interviewing for a role in an industrial environment – then dress how you would go to work. Still aim for SHARP.

This is a huge opportunity to stand out with your personality and confidence!

I have a bit of an unusual style which is distinctly me. From my crazy-ass hair to the big jewelry – it is all part of my personal brand. Which on the great news side, people tend to remember me!

(And, yes, I'm always asked – there is a mastermind guy behind my crazy locks – his name is Adam and he's been my go-to guy for a decade.)

So, go with your style.

Sharp Details Make The Difference.
And Make You Sharper.

Remember the last time you bought a car?

You went over that baby with a fine tooth comb before you bought it.

You checked for every little detail that showed you how this car has been taken care of.

Well. You're a car. Or maybe a big-assed half-ton...

They show that you *pay attention to detail* and you look at the *bigger picture* as well.

- Shoes must be shone. And not making any weird noises like squeaking or heels that are ground down.

- Jeans are good in lots of situations. If you're applying for a role where jeans would be acceptable to wear to work each day, then they're absolutely OK to wear to the interview. Jeans with rips fall in and out of fashion (I have a pair or two myself) however I would keep those pairs tucked away for non work events.

- Cleavage is a no-no. Corporate = covered.

- Nails must be clean. The only exception would be a mechanic. For women – if you're using polish, ensure it is free of chips, cracks and decals.

- Shirts should have sleeves – even a short sleeve. Sleeveless is just too casual.

- Flip flops – absolute NO. Unless of course you're interviewing for a job that would require you to wear them every day!

- Sunglasses should be tucked away. While a lovely fashion statement to have them on the top of your head....it is just a touch too casual for an interview.

- For the gents and gals with short hair – aim for a trim every 3 – 4 weeks to keep locks looking sharp.

- If it is raining take an umbrella. The drowned rat look just doesn't work.

- Purses go on the floor – never on the desk or interview table.

Sidebar story: A few years ago I met with a candidate who looked like she'd literally walked out of the shower. It was pouring rain out – I'm not sure how far away she parked, but between the water dripping off her hair and on the floor along with her soaked clothing, she only had a quarter of my attention! And, that was *after* I suggested that she zip to the washroom to dry off before we started the interview.

Moral of the story: Always bring an umbrella. I'd like to focus on your shiny results vs. the drips.

A quick story on what NOT to wear.

I was interviewing for our receptionist, (who we call the Director of Awesome). I wanted to find someone who was AWESOME in every way. Attitude, personality, talent and of course an extension of our brand. It will take any candidate about 15 seconds to look at our website and figure out what the style of the team at TAG. Sharp, crisp, professional would be a couple of words to describe us. And, everyone is in a suit.

Sooooo, imagine my surprise when I went out to greet my first candidate of the day and GASP she was wearing a skort (gents, no, that isn't a typo – a skort is a skirt but with shorts underneath. It is a really quite a clever piece of clothing) and golf attire, right down to the shoes.

I didn't really care that she went golfing early in the morning.

But I did care that she wore the same clothes to our interview.

She failed within those first 7 seconds.

When you arrive to an interview, you're showing me the very best version of you.

If you come to an interview in golf attire, I can only imagine what you might wear on a casual Friday. Tank top? T-shirt? Yoga pants? Flip flops? GASP.

If you need to change out of work clothes and into interview attire, find a place to change so you're sharply dressed. If Clark Kent can turn into Superman in a phone booth, you can find a place to change into your sharp interview outfit.

Make Your 7 Seconds Count!

The Style Guys - Jason Krell & Alykhan Velji are style experts on a mission to save the world from pleated pants, Crocs and yoga attire in public. Writers, presenters and spokespeople, Jason and Aly are based in Calgary but travel the globe extensively as part of their ongoing research to discover all things style. They have a weekly segment on Virgin Radio Calgary, a bi-weekly column in 24 Hours Vancouver, and can be seen around the world on E! Network's 'Celebrity Style Story' and Cosmo TV's 'Styleography'. They are the official spokespeople for Calgary's Crossiron Mills and make regular appearances on several other television news programs.

Who better to gain insight on "dressing sharp" than from these 2 experts!

Sheila: What's the most common misstep in business attire that you see?

The Style Guys: When it comes to business attire, most people either get stuck in a rut and wear the same things for too long, or they don't add any personality into their look. It can sometimes be boring. Business attire

The Style Guys - Jason Krell, Partner, At Large Communications & Alykhan Velji, Principal, Alykhan Velji Designs.

(Photo courtesy of The Style Guys.)

doesn't equal boring. There are so many ways to add personality with accessories, patterns and textures.

Sheila: On general appearance – what do you think gets noticed when meeting someone for the first time?

The Style Guys: Overall grooming. Even if fashion is not your top priority, regular haircuts, morning primping and properly cared for clothes goes a long way. If any of these things are missing - it's difficult to see past.

Sheila: What are you top 3 recommendations for dressing sharp?

The Style Guys:
1. **Mix it up.** Try a pant suit instead of a skirt and blazer. Or wear a dress with a blazer to mix things up.

2. **Add colour.** Wearing a bold colour will make you stand out. It shows confidence and that you are comfortable in taking risks.

3. **Wear a pattern.** Patterns and textures make outfits more dynamic and less boring. Extra points for mixing patterns - this really elevates a look.

Sheila: What advice would you give on dressing sharp for an interview?

The Style Guys: Be confident in your look for an interview. The last thing you want is to be wearing something you are not comfortable in because it will show. Wear your best, most confident look to show them what you are made of. Good fashion sense says a lot about you.

Sheila: Thoughts on fragrance?

The Style Guys: We are big fans of fragrance but never over due it. Wear something subtle, something that you have had a lot of compliments on. And always be sure if the office you are entering has a fragrance-free policy or not.

Thanks Style Guys! Great advice. **And, seriously, *how cool do these two look in the photo*?**

There you have it. Everything you need to know to make your 7 seconds count and how to dress sharp.

"Dressing well is a form of good manners."

— TOM FORD

CHAPTER 10

4 RARE Occasions When It's OK To Cancel An Interview.

Oh noooooooooooooooooooooooooo.

You've done all this work to finally be invited to the interview. It is set and now you can't make it.

You don't know what to do and heart rate is in the red zone?

Don't worry.

The 4 RARE Occasions You Can Cancel An Interview:

1. You're SICK.

I mean GREEN, incoherent and the only place you should be is in your BED. If you can only bring germs and not your A game. Stay home. Postpone the interview.

We've seen way too many go-getter candidates go to their interview and BLOW it because their energy and enthusiasm are low. And, when we ask what the heck happened in the interview, they say,

"Oh, I'm really ill, and I guess I didn't bring my A game."

You're right. If you don't bring it, you don't get the job.

2. Something RATTLES you to the core.

A stellar candidate was about to walk into her first interview with our client. She took a phone call with some terrible news about a family member. She was shaken and devastated. But, she walked into the interview with her head in that terrible news and blew it. The interview lasted no more than 20 minutes. And, the door on that gig was firmly closed.

She should have called us to ask that the meeting be rescheduled.

Points for showing up for both of these scenarios – BUT, because they weren't fully in the interview head space, they lost out on the opportunity.

3. You're going to be LATE.

This one could go either way. Being late is usually just poor planning. If there's a major traffic disruption, snow storm or other reason causing a major delay for EVERYONE, then it can be OK.

Call the hiring manager or recruiter. If you're going to be more than 10 minutes late, it will be best to reschedule.

If it is just poor planning, you may not get a second chance.

4. Silly things happen.

Loads of silly things can happen. You get in the car and split your pants. Your pen explodes on your white shirt. Your heel breaks off. All sorts of things can happen. I'd rather you cancel than see more of you than I'd like – or see you not at your best. If I took a call from a candidate who had the sense of humour to share a moment – I'd giggle for sure and gladly re-schedule.

Stuff happens...

It sure does. I'll share one of my "silly moments". This is what my eyebrow looked like after my head came in contact with my front closet door en route to the office one morning. I called my team to say that I'd be in as soon as I stopped the bleeding...5 stitches later I arrived at the office. You just have to chuckle when silly human stuff happens. Own it. Find the humour and move on with your day.

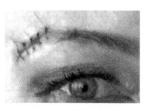

"Every time you find humour in a situation, you win."
— SNOOPY

If the STUFF causes you to not be fully present in the interview - be honest, call and reschedule. Most hiring managers appreciate honesty and will likely reschedule.

When it's NOT cool to cancel an interview:

The day of the interview.   Unless it's for one of the rare reasons I just mentioned.

If a candidate cancels an interview with me an hour or minutes before the scheduled time, they are going to hit my **#shit** list.

The best thing you can do when offered an interview is to GO.

Even if you aren't sure about the GIG, *go to the interview*.

1. You might learn more about the role in the interview and realize it is an AMAZING role.

2. The hiring manager might have another role in mind for you that isn't advertised.

3. There might be another connection to the manager for an even better role within another department or company.

4. The role you interviewed for might not be a fit, but the PERFECT role comes up with that manager in the coming months. You'll be on speed dial once it comes in.

5. You might end up with an hour with a recruiter (like me) who'll give you an hour of intensive resume and interview coaching that's a game changer.

The point is – you just never know what unexpected, fabulous outcomes might arise.

Don't over-analyze and don't be a chicken.

It is an hour of your time. Just GO.

"80% of success is showing up."

— WOODY ALLEN

CHAPTER 11
Follow Up to be a Stand-Out

"Better to be a nerd than one of the herd!"
— MANDY HALE

You know all those manners your mom tried to drill into you?

Keep your elbows off the table.
Don't chew with your mouth open.
Look someone in the eye when you shake their hand.
Always take your plate to the sink.
Stand up straight.
Say please and thank you.
Speak when you enter a room.

Mom Betty always reminded me as a kid to sit and be quiet (and be good) when we were out visiting. Oh, and sit up straight too. Mom and I giggled when I refreshed her memory on a story. (PS – This is Mom Betty.)

I recall being about 4 or 5 years old. We were out visiting one of my parent's friends. This friend had the hippest house I'd ever seen. White shag carpet, white leather furniture – this place looked like it fell out of a magazine. So, there I sat quietly beside my mom as I listened to the adults chat.

Imagine how freaked out I was when I was presented with a giant glass of GRAPE juice.

OMG, was she kidding? I was 5. I spilled stuff. All-the-time.

Chances were if I put my little sandwich grabbers on that glass of purple juice, it would likely just explode all over the beautiful white shag carpet.

Sooooo, my 5 year old interpretation of good manners was to just ignore it was even sitting there. To this day, it still makes me laugh. It could have been a disaster! So, a good choice. (Even though I really wanted the grape juice!)

Whether you're 5 or 50 – manners count.

Following Up Properly Is NICE and It Shows You're A Class Act

Following up after an interview is simply nice etiquette. And good manners are always in style.

My top pick for standing out is to send a *hand written card*.

Old school? Sure.

It's an easy way to be memorable.

It's almost never done. Be a nerd – send a card.

Thank you cards stay on our desks for a very long time. Actually, we glanced around the office and some of the thank you cards have been displayed for close to a year.

That's a sign of how RARE it is.

It's a good idea for you to zip back to our experts' section and take note of how many of our experts mentioned follow up.

OK, what should you say in a thank you card?

Dear Sheila,

Thank you so much your time on Tuesday afternoon. I really enjoyed our conversation and learning more about TAG Recruitment and the role with your firm. I am excited to hear from you on the next steps in the selection process. It was really nice to meet you in person.

Very best,

Mary

This tells me you're trying to be a stand out. I like stand outs.

A follow up email is also a good choice to follow up. It doesn't have the same stand-out factor as a card, but it works too. The card or email should be written and sent the same day as the interview.

MOST candidates don't follow up AT ALL after the first interview.

As noted in Chapter 8, you should always find out the timeframe for next steps at the end of the interview. Once that timeframe has passed, it's absolutely OK to follow up with a phone call or follow up email.

"An opportunity is missed by most people because it is dressed in overalls and looks like work."
— THOMAS A. EDISON

I always invite candidates to follow up with me. **Most don't.**

Why?

It takes some effort.

You'll have to make note of the agreed follow up date and *actually follow up* with a phone call or email.

For some it feels too pushy.

You might be thinking, "Well, if they were interested in me, they'd follow up with me."

Not always true. The hiring manager can simply be snowed under with other priorities. The recruiter might be off with another more pressing priority. Lots of things can take a hiring decision or timeline off course.

Follow up shows initiative – it isn't pushy, unless you *turn into a stalker*. (More on how-not-to-be-a-stalker in the next few pages.)

At every stage of the interview process, you're showing an employer how you'd perform as an employee. If you don't follow up, you're telling me that you'll likely not follow up properly in your daily routine if hired.

And, that's not good.

You want to use following up as a GREAT opportunity to stand out with your communication style and to show consistency.

It also gives you the chance to show your *resilience* in handling the comment:

"...thanks for following up, I don't have an answer for you yet".

This isn't the time for showing any attitude.

It's the time to be gracious, understanding and conversational. Ask when it would be appropriate to follow up again. That'll get you top marks.

"Life is short, but there is always time for courtesy."
— RALPH WALDO EMERSON

5 Things To Do When Following Up Via Phone:

1. Use your first and last name.
2. Remind the hiring manager when you met and the role you're interviewing for.
3. Indicate you're checking in on both the status of the role and timing of next steps.
4. Be **positive** in your tone. If the role has been delayed, simply ask when you should follow up again.
5. Thank the hiring manager for taking your call (or returning your call if leaving a message).

#1 above might seem silly. Wait till you hear this story!

It Was The Multiple Mike Show!

I interviewed 5 candidates on one day ALL with the first name of Mike.

Imagine when I got a series of voice mails from the various Mikes all following up on their interview and status, using only the name, **"Mike"**. GRIN. Mike who?

So please share your last name too!

Caution: Avoid Stalking the Interviewer

I was working with a candidate who called me one morning 9 times.

Yes, 9! I was on a long conference call and counted the number of times his call came in.

He went from a strong candidate, to a little bit of a *crazy one*. Thank goodness he was coachable and learned the value of leaving a concise voice mail message, rather than keeping me on speed dial.

"It takes 24 hours to 2 weeks to hear from the company with their decision."
— Jacquelyn Smith, Forbes

During the first interview, the hiring steps should be outlined along with the time-frame. If it isn't, it's a GREAT question to ask at the interview. If there are delays along the way, simply ask in each conversation *when* would be a good timeframe to follow up again.

We'd all love hiring decisions to be made faster. If there are delays, use your conversations or voice mails as a way to continue to make a great impression. The undertone of what you're sharing with your future company is valuable.

You're demonstrating 5 things that can keep you in the running:

1. You have consistent follow up and you call/email when asked.

2. Your professionalism and communication skills are consistent.

3. You can roll with the punches. You understand that delays happen.

4. You're standing out amongst others vying for the same role.

5. You're developing a further relationship with the Hiring Manager.

    Keep consistent with your follow up and you WILL stand out.

But don't call 9 times in 1 day. Just say NO to 9.

CHAPTER 12

You've got the GIG. Now Negotiate.

Yaaaay! They like you. They want you. Now it's time to **talk turkey**.

This can be a scary part. You don't want to go too high. Nor do you want to take an offer that's too low.

"Unless you know what you want, you can't ask for it."

-JEANNE SEGAL, PH.D

In the old days it was a *silly dance*.

Candidates would always say,

"Make me an offer based on my experience."

That was DUMB.

It's like dancing without any music. You have no idea whether it is a salsa, tango or a two-step.

You're just going to **GUESS.**

And, when the music comes on after you've started to bust a move, chances are you'll look silly doing a tango to country music.

Let's make sure you don't make that mistake.

I ask candidates 2 simple questions on salary:

1. **Tell me where your compensation is now.**
2. **Where would you ideally like to be in your next role?**

(And, I'll also tell you if you're too low or too high in your expectations.)

If you're honest with those 2 questions, you'll be on your way to helping a future employer make a reasonable offer.

Yes, it's normal to look for an increase when moving to another role. You're not jumping ship to just get a longer lunch break.

10 Big Things For You To Consider for Compensation:

1. **Base annual salary.**
   a. What is the base salary in comparison to where you are now?

2. **Benefits package:**
   a. Is it fully or partially paid by the company?
   b. What's covered?
   c. When does it start? Is it right away or after a waiting period?
   NOTE: Don't add the value of your benefits package to your salary. That just muddies the water. Keep salary and benefit separate.

3. **Bonus structure:**
   a. How is it earned?
   b. When is it paid?
   c. What % has been paid in the past?
   d. Is it achievable?

4. **Vacation:**
   a. How many weeks annually?
   b. Is vacation earned and eligible to be taken in the first year?
   c. When does the number of weeks increase?

5. **Personal days or sick days?**
   a. Are they offered?
   b. How many?
   c. Is there a waiting period?

6. **Allowances:**
   a. Cell
   b. Car
   c. Mileage reimbursement
   d. Travel expenses (per diem)
   e. Parking

7. **Training and Professional Development:**
    a. Tuition reimbursement
    b. Membership in your professional association
    c. Professional Development courses

8. **Pension & Investments:**
    a. RRSP matching
    b. Stock purchase or matching

9. **Fun stuff:**
    a. This one is a fun one at my company. You'll get a nice gift certificate and team lunch on your birthday.
    b. How are milestones celebrated? At TAG this is a big one. When we hit financial thresholds, we hop in a cab and zip downtown for a lingering lunch at our favourite hot spot. And, one milestone was celebrated with Betty's buns. Yes, my Mom arrived with pans of her famous buns for lunch!
    c. Is there extra time off for the Holidays?
    d. Do you receive the Civic Holidays in addition to the Statutory Holidays?

10. **Other stuff:**
    a. What is the start/end time?
    b. Is it a 37.5 or 40 hour work week?
    c. Travel time to and from work?
    d. Work environment?

So Now You Have An Offer But It Feels A Little Light/Wishy-Washy?

They like you. They want you. And now they've offered you something that just isn't going to do it for you.

You don't want to offend them but you know you can't accept it either.

2 Safe Questions To Ask BEFORE You Sweat Through A Negotiation:

1. **Is the offer firm?**

2. **Do we have any room to move?**

Keep to the facts.

Example:

I'm currently at a total income of XX with base and bonus with XX weeks of vacation. To make a move, I do need to be at XX.

And don't apologize for it.
Don't make excuses.
Don't fumble and flop around.

Make your statement with confidence.

2 Negotiation No- No's:

1. You've given your number on where you'd like to be.... and then you change your mind and drastically increase what you'd like for annual salary. This usually kills a negotiation.

2. Opening up the conversation after you've signed the offer. The deal is done when you sign.

P.S. It's OK to decline an offer if the numbers don't work. Treat it in the same manner as resigning. By doing it in a professional manner, and declining an offer with class - it will always make you memorable.

Send them a thank-you card.

Your mother would be happy if you did that.

CHAPTER 13
How to Resign Like A Pro

5 Rules for Breaking Up

I know, I know.

Breaking up is so hard to do in both personal and professional relationships.

You want it to be a break up not a blow- up. No dynamite.

Listen.

You made the decision to look for a new position and thought *that* was the tough part.

But there's one more step.

For many people, the hardest part of making the move to a new job is the resignation. Break ups are never easy.

Some of course dream of that moment of telling their former boss some precise reasons for leaving, and many dwell on how wonderful it might be. GRIN.

But this isn't the time for you to be aggressive or tell your boss where to go. Resign with grace. Always.

Work hard and keep focused during your notice period. You'll very likely someday need a reference from your manager. Being respectful, hard working and professional right to the end of your last day keeps you in the good books.

Think about ways you'd *never* want to be dumped personally. The same rules apply in breaking up with your company.

You wouldn't want to be dumped by someone via technology:

Make A Wish

When you're on opposite pages and never knew it.

Ways *not* to break up using technology:

- Text message
- Sticky note
- Voice mail
- Email

Don't let technology make you a coward with your boss either.

Think about the **TIMING** - you'd never want to be dumped on a Friday night. OK, well maybe that would be a good thing as you'd have your weekend free!

When is the best time to do the deed?

Resignations are best done on a **Monday morning**.

Your manager then has the full week ahead to get his/her plan in place on how to allocate your work, cross train and find your replacement.

And, the **LOCATION** – you'd probably want to be in private, not in the middle of a theatre performance or in a restaurant if you were dumping or being dumped personally.

Resignations are best in your manager's office or board room for a private conversation.

I've had my fair share of employee BREAK UPS. Most were done professionally. But, I have a few FUN stories to share of what NOT to do.

1. The Drifting Off Into The Sunset Approach

One of my recruiters knew he wasn't making the grade and it was obvious I was going to be scheduling THE conversation at any time. He left that afternoon, said goodbye and the usual, "See you tomorrow".

I walked by his office a short time later to see his office key left on his desk, personal items removed and I never heard from him again.

2. The Down To The HOUR Resignation

Another funny one (in retrospect) was a recruiter who calculated what she thought she was owed for sick days, vacation and all sorts of other weird things – right to the hour.

She resigned on a Wednesday at 1 PM and calculated her notice down to the hour. Yes, she was leaving on Friday of that week at 11 AM. That one still makes me giggle.

3. The "I'm Giving You NOTICE That I'll Be RESIGNING" Notice

I received a text at 7AM on a Monday morning saying, "We really need to talk today."

Just as in a personal relationship, the phrase:

We really need to TALK is code for "we're breaking up."

5 Rules for Breaking up Professionally:

1. Letter of Resignation: We're done.

It should be professional, positive and include the notice period being provided and the date of your last day being worked.

Being gracious is always in style.

Thank your company for the time, learning, support and opportunity they've provided you. It will be appreciated.

Keep It Professional & Brief. You're Not Writing A Soap Opera Here.

It should be on a blank piece of white paper – NEVER on company letterhead. Your message is from you, not a message from the company.

Sign the letter. Place it in a blank white letter sized envelope.

Example resignation:

Dear Stella,

Please accept this letter as my formal resignation from ABC company. My last day will be _____.

I am very grateful for the extensive professional development and support that you have given me over the past five years. I have appreciated your support, mentoring and guidance in shaping my career.

Very best,

Bob Smith

2. Notice period: Elvis will be leaving the building.

Personal break ups are best handled like ripping off a band-aid. We're done. . Just done. Over. Finito. No notice required.

Professional break ups DO have notice periods based on the amount of time you've been with the company.

Less than 1 year: 1 week of working notice.

Greater than 1 year: 2 weeks of working notice.

Loads of candidates feel they'll be leaving their employer in a huge lurch if only 2 weeks is given. **Not so.**

Where's your head and heart after you've given your notice? It is with your new company.

It becomes difficult, even for the most discerning professional to keep their focus and output at a high level for more than 2 weeks.

If you have vacation owing, it will be paid out. Don't be sneaky and try to use sick pay and vacation time as part of your notice.

The notice period should be working time.

Notice is also intended to give your manager time to reassign duties to the team, do cross training and hire a replacement. This takes time.

3. Mum's the word: Repeat. **ZIP thy LIPS.**

The first person you tell is your manager.

After the conversation, a formal announcement is made by the company.

As we'll review in the next chapter on counter-offers – you might be surprised with a solution from your manager. How silly will you look in accepting a counter after you shared with everyone that you're resigning?

4. The Resignation Conversation: We're done. But can we chat?

Either make an appointment or approach your manager when you know they can give you their undivided attention.

Every manager out there knows when an employee walks in to their office and closes the door behind them with an envelope in hand – it's a RESIGNATION conversation.

Chances are you won't even have to say, "I'm leaving."

Expect QUESTIONS.

Where are you going?

What is the role?

Can you share with me why you chose to move on?

Would you leave this confidentially between us for a day or so to let me come back to you with some ideas?

5. Spill the beans:

Do share where you're going. If you're going to a competitor, your employer may choose to have you depart immediately.

If it is not a competitor – expect to work out your notice.

Leaving on positive terms is how you want to leave your organization – the world is small, and getting smaller each day, so one just never knows what paths might cross again!

And you'll always be remembered for being a class act.

CHAPTER 14
The Counter Offer – Let's Not Break Up

You've invested a lot of time into finding a new *Zippy Gig*.

You're probably feeling pretty good about yourself and it shows.

You've been through a lot to get to this point:

- Resume writing.
- Searching for that *zippy new gig*.
- Preparing for and going through the first, second, third interviews.
- Reaching out and prepping your references.
- You've bitten your nails waiting on interview feedback

And then a JOB OFFER is extended.

YAHOOOOOOO!

You're excited, scared, nervous and happy. It feels RIGHT. It's time to make a move.

You've carefully planned your RESIGNATION.

The letter has been drafted.

You're in your boss's office (likely with your voice shaking, heart rate up and palms sweaty) – the conversation has taken place, the letter has been handed over...

And then the unexpected happens...a **COUNTER OFFER** is proposed.

They don't want you to go.

Why?

They like you. They really, really like you!

The timing might suck for the company, your manager and the team.

There might be a big project about to hit and they need you.

Maybe you were about to get a promotion?
Whatever the reason, they don't want to break up.

Their counter offer is completely unexpected – and hits you completely off guard.

You decided you wanted a new gig...

Or have you?

Old Jeans vs. New Jeans: A New Way To Look At Counter Offers

You've pulled out the old favorite pair.

You put them on and (GASP) they just didn't fit quite right. Maybe a bit too tight. Perhaps too short. Or too saggy in the ass. They just didn't make you happy. You folded them back up again and put them back in the closet.

You then found yourself out at the mall in search for jeans that make you SMILE. We all know when we've found THAT pair of jeans that give you a bit of SASS. (Yes, I'm talking to the gents here too.)

They look good. Feel good. Likely you get a double take or GRIN or two as a nod of approval from the sales person.

The jeans are AMAZING. You dash to the cashier to complete your purchase. Excited, you zip home to try them on again and you start planning how these amazing new jeans are going to fit into your wardrobe.

And then. You spot your old jeans in your closet.

Two things can happen.

You try those old jeans on and they feel AMAZING - like finding an old friend. They just fit. Maybe you've been working out and they fit perfectly.

OR

They feel old, worn, out of style and don't fit like they used to. And, they don't make you happy.

Your old company might be like that old pair of jeans. Either you still fit with your old company or it just doesn't fit any longer.

And now with the counter offer you have a decision to make.

A Counter Offer Can Take Many Forms:

- More money/bonuses/holidays/perks
- A change in work area - from the cubicle by the bathroom to the nice one in the corner with a view
- A position title change
- Additional training to get you ready for a new role
- A mapped out career plan for future growth
- Formal career mentoring
- Share options

For most, a counter offer is responded to with a "thanks, but no thanks."

But to some candidates, it may be *very tempting*.

3 Things To Ponder Before You Respond:

1. Remember why you were looking for a new job in the first place.

Look at your list of the reasons WHY you're seeking a move from your present employer. You need to understand what would keep you in your current job and also
why you're seeking a move.

Think back to Chapter 1 – the REASONS why you're seeking a new *zippy gig*:

     a. More responsibility
     b. More money
     c. Environment/conditions stink.
     d. More balance with work/home.
     e. Not the right role – not a great fit with the people or company.

2. Does the counter offer fix all of the reasons you were seeking a move?

Has the core reason you were looking for a new job been addressed?

Is the new job you've just secured worth giving up?

3. Never make the decision on the spot.

If you find yourself in a situation where you walked into your manager's office to resign
and find yourself in a counter offer situation where you're contemplating the offer –
do this.

Give Yourself 24 Hours To Think.

Don't feel compelled to make a decision on the spot.

Take some time to ponder what the counter offer means to you.

"My knight in shining armor turned out to be a loser in aluminum foil"

— UNKNOWN

My friend Chris Day is the very talented Business Development Director with KPMG Enterprise. He's been with KPMG since 2007. Except for a brief loser-in-aluminum foil experience that lasted 42 business days before returning to KPMG.

I'm delighted that he's allowed me to share his incredible story.

He resigned from his role at KPMG with extreme grace. He parted ways with his firm in the most positive way.

They didn't want to breakup.
They wanted to keep him BADLY.
. He made up his mind to depart.
They respected that.
He left.

Chris: My new boss called me on the first day of my new gig to check in. I'm sure he could tell before I could that it wasn't the right fit for me.

By day 2 in my new role I had a bad feeling in my gut.

By day 10 I suspected the new organization had values and practises that were not in alignment to mine.

However, coming from a place like KPMG where the values and conduct are frankly beyond reproach, I rationalized that this was simply a "re-culturization". In other words, I have to give myself more time to get used to them. Further, I was working in a remote office, so I did not have contact with my direct boss for several days at a time. And, much of the first weeks were spent in external industry training.

By day 20 I was very concerned that I had made a really bad choice. Not being one to give up, I figured it best to carry on and give this my absolute best.

Nope, day 40 I was sure this "new" organization was not good. They have values and practices that were simply not acceptable.

I could never be proud of them.

I could never allow them anywhere near my relationship inventory.

I did not like them and they did not like me. Perfect.

I was sure. I resigned that day.

Thankfully my relationship with KPMG was as strong as it was on exit. And all during this time, we connected on a regular basis – in person meetings, industry events and phone contact. I had lunch with my old boss along with email and phone contact with other team members. Our communication never stopped.

Sheila: What went through your mind when you realized that the company you joined wasn't quite what you'd signed up for – the "oh no" moment?

Chris: That I had put my family and my career at risk. How could I have so easily misread their true values? I was very disappointed in myself for not seeing who they really were. In hindsight, I know now that I allowed myself to see what I wanted to see at the time. And, I should have quit on the spot on day 2 and listened to my gut, right there, right then. That would be the only mulligan that I would ask for in that whole experience.

Sheila: What was it like to walk back into your old office those few months later?

Chris: It was like I had never left. The team was in full welcome back mode. My project folders were still on the shared drive, same phone number and of course they kept my KPGM Enterprise business cards. Many clients and future clients did not even know that I was on a "career sabbatical" for 42 business days. The team made me feel welcome....and in the first hours back, I could frankly carry right on from where I left off.

Thank you for sharing your story Chris!

Take note.

Chris did absolutely everything right. He resigned with extreme grace. He worked diligently to his last day with KPMG. He maintained his professional relationships. The result – he was invited back with open arms.

When Is It OK To Accept A Counter Offer?

1. Your manager offers a solution you didn't even think was a possibility.

I had a very long term employee who came into my office with tears in her eyes as she handed over the dreaded letter.

Cindy's husband had secured a job in another city.

She had to resign as they were moving.

In a split second, I said,

> "Well, why don't you just work remotely from the new city?"

We both GRINNED with excitement.

There WAS a solution. She didn't have to resign. We were both thrilled.

Listen to the solution. Give yourself time to think and ponder.

2. Show me THE Money.

You love everything about your job.
You LOVE your co-workers, clients, and environment.
You love everything.

But you need to be earning more. There's no doubt about it.

If you're in this situation, I STRONGLY suggest you have a conversation with your manager *well before* you start a new job search.

Perhaps there's a pay for performance solution or a change in job duties that could result in higher pay and you being happier.

If money is the only stickler and a solution can be found, it would be a GREAT reason to accept a counter offer.

3. You have a Loser-in-Aluminum-Foil experience.

The gig you went to wasn't what you thought it would be. It was a mistake. You can feel it in your gut.

If you resigned professionally, like Chris, that door might be wide open for you to return.

If the counter offer feels right, chances are it is. Going back to your former role, as Chris did OR staying put to accept the counter offer can be a great decision. Only you will know if staying put or moving on is the right move.

Give yourself time to ponder both options. You should be flattered. You've got two great options to consider.

Lucky you!

CHAPTER 15

Social Media & Your *Zippy Gig*

Yes, *of course* we look. Everyone looks.

Yet it surprises me how many people think that employers and recruiters aren't bothering to check you out on social media.

If you've made the 11 second cut – you can bet we're cruising through social media at some point through the interview process.

You want to keep your image professional and clean to ensure you get the *zippy gig*.

"Social media doesn't create negativity, it uncovers it."
SETH GODIN

LinkedIn: 5 Rules About Your Photo:

1. Photo must be a professional head shot.

It doesn't have to be a formal one taken by a photographer, but it needs to show your business persona.

For the gents – you need to be wearing a shirt. No beach pictures.

For the gals – it needs to look like you are wearing a shirt. GRIN.

If you were photographed at the holiday party in a fabulous strapless dress and you crop to only have your head and shoulders...well, honey it looks like you're not wearing anything. Zip on over to **Chapter 9** on dressing sharp for a refresh and some recommendations.

You shouldn't be holding any type of cocktail. Unless that's your job.

2. The photo should only be of YOU.

The pics with your cat, dog, college pals, spouse, kids or the like go on Facebook. LinkedIn is all about showing you as the professional business person.

3. Yes, you need a photo.

If I see a profile without a photo, I always think, "Hmmm, wonder why?"

4. The photo should be your business face.

 No sultry, sexy looks. This isn't the site to get dates. Well, I guess you could, but that shouldn't be the objective.
No sunglasses. Unless you work on a beach.

5. The photo should look like you.

When I meet you, I should be able to recognize you. It should be current.

What To Put In Your LinkedIn Profile?

Easy.

Simply copy your shiny new resume and insert into LinkedIn.

Facebook: 2 Must-do's:

1. **Lock your privacy settings.**

2. **Or keep your photos and posts fun and clean.**

<u>**Or even better, do both.**</u>

Remember, we look.

And, yes, job offers have been halted because of questionable comments or photos on Facebook.

Remember – you reveal your personality and values in pretty much everything you do.

And sometimes what may look like an innocent post – has revealed your real intentions.

Sidebar story: We were working with a candidate on a very key role for a growing organization. Critical to the hiring manager was having someone she could count on to be with the organization for the next 3 – 5 years. While there was no guarantee of course, they just wanted a strong probability that the successful candidate would be there for the longer term.

Here's what happened.

The interviews were a success. Her references were stellar. An offer was being drafted. And, then....

The hiring manager checked the candidate's previous posts. There it was. A simple comment stopped the deal in its tracks. She had posted that she was thinking about going back to university to pursue an advanced degree in the fall.

BOOM.

Done. Offer was sent to the recycle bin.

As innocent as it was, it cost her the gig. No offer. No further conversation. It was over.

"93% of hiring managers will review a candidate's social media profile before making a decision."

"55% have reconsidered a candidate based on what they find."

SOURCE: MONEY — OCTOBER 16, 2014

Social Media: A Chat With An Expert

I chatted with Sean Sandhurst, Manager Social Media Strategy, Postmedia Network Inc. to gain his perspective.

Sheila: What tips would you give to candidates in using social media for research on companies?

Sean: Social media allows the candidate a massive amount of information at their fingertips:

- Insights into the organization and corporate culture
- Insights into employees and how you might be connected to them
- Connecting with people within an industry to build a relationship and gather information

Sean: It is also very insightful to look at a prospective company that you are interviewing with and observe what they post about. What social channels are they active on? Does what you see on social media resonate with your core values? Use social media to get an inside-look at the organization which can provide insight into the company, products, announcements, etc. You can also follow companies that you want to work for to get updates from their social posts.

Sheila: What tips would you recommend to candidates on their personal social media presence?

Sean: While a candidate searches for their perfect job, they also need to showcase their best-self on social media channels and use them to build your personal brand.

One thing to start with is to review your name on a Google search, using a Chrome browser extension called "Incognito". It will help you to see what others may see when they search for your name. Look at your social channels through the eyes of a recruiter or boss. Ask yourself what message am I sending the public with my social media posts. Is it professional? Would someone want to hire me?

The next step is to review your Facebook privacy settings. Review your timeline, news feeds and any other public facing posts. Hide and/or delete ones that you might not want a future manager to see.

LinkedIn is a personal billboard and in effect, the resume of the CV of the present. It is a living resume, listing skills, competencies, recommendations, endorsements and examples of your work. Ensure the public-facing information is what you want people to know about you. Do ask for recommendations from former colleagues, bosses, or customers helps to build a story about yourself.

Sheila: Any last recommendations?

Sean: One thing to remember that anything that is on the internet about you, reflect upon your brand – good, bad or ugly. Make sure you build your personal brand in a professional, respectful way that will boost your career.

Thank you for your insight Sean! You've given some great tips on how to use social media for researching prospective new employers as well as great insight into how to keep your on line presence professional.

Are You Invisible On Line?

Perhaps you hate social media. Or you're a very private person.

I get it.

BUT in today's world – if you don't have a social media presence, or some form of on-line presence – you're considered to be invisible.

Invisible means old-school.
Out of date.
Out of touch.

According to a 2015 survey from *CareerBuilder* of more than 2000 employees:

35% of employers say they're *less likely* to interview candidates if they're <u>unable</u> to *find information* about them on line.

Social Media Tools for your *Zippy Gig* Search:

1. Become a Facebook fan of the organizations you're interested in.

Yes, I'd love it if you'd follow us – TAG Recruitment Group. We post all sorts of fun stuff. *Zippy gigs* we're working on. Interview and resume tips. Silly stuff about us. Photos. (And, of course if you're a fan that doesn't mean that we're friends. So, you can see us, but we can't see you.)

2. LinkedIn:

Follow the organizations on LinkedIn. Their updates will appear in your news feed. It's a great way to keep up to date on the organization.

Review the job postings tab. You can see if you might be connected to the original poster or know someone who can introduce you.

The world of social media is changing at a quick pace. There are lots of other platforms out there which are carving a place for job searching. I've focused on the two most popular platforms....at the moment.

"We love social media because it exists at the intersection of humanity and technology."

SETH GODIN

CHAPTER 16

Dumb Things People Say. You Never Will.

I had lots of fun and many giggles writing this chapter. Each and every dumb thing written in this chapter has been said – lots of times.

If you've poured a martini for this chapter – there's a *spill warning*.

This is a chapter of BLOOPERS I don't want you to make.

There are some silly and over-used expressions to drop.

1. I have 10 years of experience *under my belt*.

> I don't want to think about what's "under your belt".
> The belt holds your pants up.
> No need to talk about your belt.

2. I bring 5 years of customer service *to the table*.

> Bring wine to the table.
> Bring potatoes to the table.
> Bring dishes to the table.
> Bring salads to the table.

Leave the table out of it.

3. I will return your call at *my earliest convenience.*

You're saying,

"I'll return your damn call, when I have absolutely nothing else to do and only when it's convenient for me. Which, quite honestly, could be never." (SMILE)

This conversation still makes my head spin.

Sheila: Good Afternoon, Sheila Musgrove speaking.

Bruce: Oh, yes Sheila, it's Bruce calling about one of your positions.

Sheila: Hi Bruce.

Bruce: It said to call Sheila or Rachel. So I'm calling. I guess you are Sheila? (Ummm, yes, that's how I answered the phone. With my name.)

Sheila: Yes, I'm Sheila....and it is Rachelle.

Bruce: Oh, right Rachelle.

Sheila: What questions can I answer for you?

Bruce: Well, I'm looking at an ad – it's pretty vague. It doesn't say what industry or product or...

Sheila: Yes, that is on purpose. Our client is in a very narrow industry vertical. Once we have your resume in hand, we can then share a lot more detail about the role. Have you sent your resume?

Bruce: Well if it is selling ballet uniforms, it probably isn't for me.

Sheila: We are pretty good at reading resumes and seeing where there might be a fit.

Bruce: Well, and I don't do photocopiers either.

Sheila: It is not in that industry.

Bruce: Well, is it in construction?

Sheila: No. It's in technical space with an emphasis on marketing.

Bruce: Oh.

Sheila: The best thing you can do to start a conversation with us is to send your resume. Have you applied?

Bruce: No. I wanted to know what role it was for.

Sheila: We disclose our client once we have a resume in hand and we are having a conversation.

Bruce: No, as much as you are screening me, I'm screening you.

Sheila: Understand. We are reviewing resumes this afternoon and tomorrow as we have a very quick turnaround on this role.

Bruce: Oh geez, I was thinking that I could get a resume to you in a week or so.

Sheila: OK, do send when you are ready.

We are now about 4 minutes into the call. And, this guy is wasting my time.

Bruce: I don't seem to see your email address. Let me just take a look see here.

Sheila : In the interests of time, let me give you my email address it's Sheila@hideseekfind.com

Bruce: (Scrambling for a pen...) Oh, um –

Sheila: Sheila@hideseekfind.com I'll watch for your resume. (....so I can send it to the shredder.)

The very best thing that you can do when you see a job that's of interest is to apply. *GRIN*

AND

If you call. Have questions. Better yet, make them SMART questions.

Worst voice mail of the day:

Candidate: Hi Mark. Call me back. 403-291-2234.

He left Mark **OUR** office number, not his phone number. Haaaaaaaaaaa.

No name and no phone number.

Really.

 SASSY Sheila advice warning.

OK. There are things you should know before leaving a voice mail:

1. Your FIRST and LAST name. We often giggle about this one.

Hi it's Mary? The sentence shouldn't sound like a question OR that you're unsure if that's really your name. Grin.

Hi, it's Mary. Call me back. Ummm, Mary of no last name. Even if I met you yesterday, leave me a last name.

Hi, it's Mary Robinson. Ahhh, that's all that you have to say. *Confidently* know both your first and last name.

2. Your phone number. Know it off the top of your head. Always repeat your phone number in a voice mail. And, leave your number *not my number*. Grin.

3. The position you're calling about. OH, we have lots of funny examples on this one.

I'm calling about the job on the computer.

I'm calling about a position you posted last week.

I'm calling about the job on the internet.

I'm calling about the job that I got an email alert on.

OK, most people can pull these details out without much rehearsal.

4. Rehearse leaving a voice mail message.

 Sassy Sassy Sheila advice:

If you're looking for a *Zippy Gig* – always answer the phone with your name. First and last.

"Sheila Musgrove speaking."

Verbal ISMS To Avoid:

Recruiters listen for a living. We pick up on some verbal isms that can be conversation and interview killers!

- Ummmm. Drop the umms – better to say nothing and let your words breathe, ratherthan stringing your thoughts together with a bunch of umms.

- Would you be the person hiring "er"? (Yes, this is an ism – it is a way, albeit a bad way to end a sentence. Rather than asking the question and leaving it at that, there is an attempt at an "or"? but it just comes off as "er". It just sounds dumb.

- "You know what I mean?" – Suddenly this has popped up as a way to sum up a conversation. My response is usually, "Yes, I do know what you mean."

- Overuse of the word, "like".

- Ending sentences with "Right?"

Have a friend listen to your speech for verbal isms...we all have something, just make sure it isn't an ism that is going to lend you a big fat no at the end of the interview!!

This chapter was intended to give you a chuckle or two.

We all have days when we say dumb things.

Words come out backwards or even jumbled.

You just have to laugh and get back on track and let your shiny, prepared results take centre stage.

Let's Recap!

Ditch the Rusty Resume.

Create a Shiny Sexy Resume Filled with Results.

Get your Phone To Ring.

Do Your Research.

Prepare.

Deliver a Kick-ass Interview.

Ask Clever Questions.

Dress Sharp.

Negotiate.

Follow Up.

Get Hired.

Enjoy Your New *Zippy Gig*!

CHAPTER 17
The End. The Beginning of Your New *Zippy Gig*

You've done it.

You've created a super shiny resume, delivered a kick-ass interview and you've landed the *Zippy Gig.*

Congratulations!

Drop me a note.

How did I do? What *Zippy* tips worked? Tell me your story. I'd love to hear from you.

Sheila@hideseekfind.com

I wish you incredible success
in your new *Zippy Gig!*

Success

what people think
it looks like

Success

what it really
looks like

Made in the USA
Charleston, SC
08 August 2016